SHIFTING INTO NEUTRAL?

Burden Sharing in the Western Alliance in the 1990s

Also from Brassey's

CAHEN
The Western European Union and NATO

COKER
Drifting Apart? The Superpowers and their European Allies

COKER
A Nation in Retreat? Britain's Defence Commitment

COKER
British Defence Policy in the 1990s: A Guide to the
Defence Debate

GROVE
NATO's Defence of the North

SLOAN
NATO in the 1990s

WILKINSON & CHICHESTER
British Defence: A Blueprint for Reform

SHIFTING INTO NEUTRAL?

Burden Sharing in the Western Alliance in the 1990s

Edited by

CHRISTOPHER COKER

BRASSEY'S (UK)

(Member of Maxwell Macmillan Pergamon Publishing Corporation)

LONDON • OXFORD • WASHINGTON • NEW YORK • BEIJING
FRANKFURT • SÃO PAULO • SYDNEY • TOKYO • TORONTO

UK (Editorial)	Brassey's (UK) Ltd., 24 Gray's Inn Road, London WC1X 8HR, England
(All orders except North America)	Brassey's (UK) Ltd., Headington Hill Hall, Oxford OX3 0BW, England
USA (Editorial)	Brassey's (US) Inc., 8000 Westpark Drive, Fourth Floor, McLean, Virginia 22102, USA
(North American Orders)	Brassey's, Front and Brown Streets, Riverside, NJ 08075, USA 800 257 5755 (Toll Free)
PEOPLE'S REPUBLIC OF CHINA	Pergamon Press, Room 4037, Qianmen Hotel, Beijing, People's Republic of China
FEDERAL REPUBLIC OF GERMANY	Pergamon Press GmbH, Hammerweg 6, D-6242 Kronberg, Federal Republic of Germany
BRAZIL	Pergamon Editora Ltda, Rua Eça de Queiros, 346, CEP 04011, Paraiso, São Paulo, Brazil
AUSTRALIA	Brassey's Australia Pty Ltd., PO Box 544, Potts Point, NSW 2011, Australia
JAPAN	Pergamon Press, 5th Floor, Matsuoka Central Building, 1-7-1 Nishishinjuku, Shinjuku-ku, Tokyo 160, Japan
CANADA	Pergamon Press Canada Ltd., Suite No. 271, 253 College Street, Toronto, Ontario, Canada M5T 1R5

Copyright © 1990 Brassey's (UK)

First edition 1990

Library of Congress Cataloging in Publication Data
Shifting into neutral?: Burden Sharing in the Western
Alliance in the 1990s edited by Christopher Coker.—1st ed.
p. cm
1. North Atlantic Treaty Organization—Finance. 2. North
Atlantic Treaty Organization—United States. 3. United
States—Military relations—Europe. 4. Europe—Military
relations—United States. I. Coker, Christopher.
UA646.3.S47 1990 355′.031′091821—dc20 89-25163

British Library Cataloguing in Publication Data
Shifting into neutral?: Burden Sharing in the Western
Alliance in the 1990s.
1. North Atlantic Treaty Organization. Role of United
States
I. Coker, Christopher
355′.031′091821

ISBN 0-08-037714-9

Printed in Great Britain by B.P.C.C. Wheatons Ltd., Exeter

Contents

About the Authors

Michael Brenner is Professor in the Graduate School of Public & International Affairs at the University of Pittsburgh. His writings on American foreign policy and international security have appeared in numerous scholarly journals, including *International Affairs, World Politics, Foreign Policy* and *International Organization*. His last book, *Nuclear Power & Non-Proliferation*, was published by Cambridge University Press. Professor Brenner has held previous academic appointments at Cornell, Stanford and the University of California.

Guy de Carmoy is Professor of International Relations at INSEAD, Fontainbleau and a Member of Staff of the Bureau of the Committee of the Standing Committee on Atlantic Organisations.

Christopher Coker has been a Lecturer in International Affairs at the London School of Economics since 1982. He is the author of several books including *British Defence Policy in the 1990s* (Brassey's 1987) and the most recent book in the SCAO series, *Drifting Apart? The Superpowers and their European Allies* (Brassey's 1989).

Lawrence S Eagleburger is US Assistant Secretary of State. Before that he was President of Kissinger Associates which he joined in 1984 after serving for twenty-seven years in the Department of State. At the State Department he held various positions including that of Secretary of State for Political Affairs (1982–84). Earlier he served as Assistant Secretary of State for European Affairs, Ambassador to Yugoslavia, Deputy Under Secretary of State for Management, Executive Assistant to Secretary of State Kissinger, Deputy Assistant Secretary of Defense and Deputy Assistant to the President for National Security Affairs.

David Garnham is Professor of Political Science at The University of Wisconsin–Milwaukee, USA. His research focuses on international conflict and defence policy. He has authored *The Politics of European Defense Co-operation: Germany, France, Britain, and America* (Ballinger 1988) and numerous articles and book chapters.

Walter Goldstein is Professor of International Relations and Public Policy at Rockefeller College, State University of New York at Albany. Formerly, he was Visiting Professor of SAIS/Bologna and Colombia. He has written frequently on NATO affairs and world trade conflicts. He is also the Editor of two books in the current series, including *Fighting Allies* (Brassey's 1986).

Dr Martin J Hillenbrand came to the University of Georgia in September, 1982 as the first Dean Rusk Professor of International Relations. Prior to that he had served since early 1977 as Director General of the Atlantic Institute for International Affairs. As a professional diplomat he served as the first US Ambassador to Hungary (1967–1969), Assistant Secretary of State for European Affairs (1969–1972) and Ambassador to the Federal Republic of Germany (1972–1976). He is author, co-author or editor of the following books: *Power and Morals* (1949); *Zwischen Politik und Ethik* (1968); *The Future of Berlin* (1980); *Global Insecurity: A Strategy for Energy and Economic Renewal* (1982) and *Germany In An Era of Transition* (1984) and is also the author of numerous articles and chapters of books.

Jim Moody served in the Congress of the United States between 1982–88. He previously served in the Wisconsin State Assembly and State Senate from 1977–82. He was a member of the Ways and Means Committee and two of its sub-committees on Health and Social Security. He was also a Congressional delegate to the US–Soviet arms reduction talks in Geneva.

Sir Frank Roberts GCMG GCVO entered the Foreign Office in 1930. British Minister in Moscow in 1945, he was Principal Private Secretary to the Secretary of State for Foreign Affairs 1947–49, HM Ambassador to Yugoslavia 1954–57, United Kingdom Permanent Representative on the North Atlantic Council 1957–60, Ambassador to the USSR 1960–62 and to the Federal German Republic 1963–68. President of the British Atlantic Committee 1968–81, the Atlantic Treaty Association 1969–73 and of the European Atlantic Group 1973–83.

Dr Steve Smith is Senior Lecturer in International Relations and Director of the Centre for Public Choice Studies at the University of East Anglia. He is Editor of the Cambridge University Press Series *Studies in International Relations* and is on the Executive of the British International Studies Association. He is author of *Foreign Policy Adaption* (1981), Editor of *International Relations* (1985) and Co-Editor of *Politics and Human Nature* (1983), *Foreign Policy Implementation* (1985), *The Cold War Past and Present* (1987), *British Foreign Policy* (1988) and *Belief Systems and International Relations* (1988).

Introduction

SIR FRANK ROBERTS

The Standing Committee on Atlantic Organisations (SCAO), founded in Bellagio (Italy) in 1973, held its fifteenth annual conference at Wingspread (USA). The original intention of its founders was to provide a modest instrument of co-ordination and mutual exchange of information for voluntary organisations committed to maintaining and developing the Atlantic Alliance and the wider Atlantic Community which this protects. The annual conferences supported by NATO and held at centres on each side of the Atlantic have been organised to promote this co-ordination, without interfering in any way with the independence of each participating group. But they have developed into fora of some forty persons for discussing among these groups and with other distinguished individual participants, who thus become individual members of SCAO, some of the main issues affecting the Atlantic Alliance, whether in the areas of East–West or of West–West relations. SCAO tries to maintain a balance between the two and of course between the study of problems affecting more directly either Europe or the United States or Canada.

SCAO has had four conferences in the USA, all thanks to the hospitality of the Johnson Foundation at Racine and one in Canada at Toronto. When we last met at Wingspread in 1985 our theme was to learn about the US scene and probable American policies after the re-election of President Reagan. In 1986 in Oslo (Norway) we learned about the problems of the Northern Flank and in 1987 in Cambridge (England) we debated the problems of getting better value for money from our national defence budgets. Gorbachev's *Perestroika* and *Glasnost* and their true significance have come into our discussions increasingly since 1985.

In 1988, we returned to the United States, some thought rashly, shortly before the Presidential Election campaign got underway, to see how America viewed its responsibilities worldwide as they affected the Atlantic Alliance. We had no regrets over this timing, which certainly did not affect the usual high quality of the American participation nor that of their contributions. The Europeans were hard put to match them, but they were, after all, at Wingspread to learn. Our Rapporteur, Christopher Coker, summed up our debates so well that I have very little to add beyond this. I was glad, but not surprised, to find that Paul Kennedy's brilliant book on the decline of empires, although it threatened at one point to monopolise discussion, did not persuade our speakers that the current United States was a potential Rome of the later Emperors, nor a state sharing the weaknesses of seventeenth century Spain, nor even, to take a rather different case, a rival in this respect to pre-Thatcher Britain.

After all, the United States' decline since 1945 has been relative to its allies in Japan and in Europe and not to its adversary the Soviet Union. The US still seems prepared to meet and be capable of meeting its international responsibilities in NATO as elsewhere, whether in defence or negotiation, although naturally more insistent than in the past on its allies doing more to share the burdens, and much more reluctant than, for example, under President Kennedy to extend its responsibilities any further.

In recent years our SCAO debates have been of sufficient interest to justify their edited publication in book form. I shall be surprised if the 1988 Wingspread volume, for which Christopher Coker is responsible, does not maintain this standard.

Let me end with a final word of warm thanks to the Johnson Foundation and to Rita Gardman in particular. If, as I hope, SCAO returns to Wingspread in future years, we shall miss her very much and we wish her well in her retirement.

July 1988

The contents of this book reflect the views expressed at the Conference of the Standing Committee of Atlantic Organisations in the Spring of 1988—a point at which the Reagan Administration in America was drawing to a close and President Gorbachev was beginning to make a substantial impression upon the world scene. Since it was compiled, the whole Eastern European scene has undergone a series of dramatic changes—changes which would have defied imagination at the time of the Conference. All are having a profound effect upon East-West relations and the structures of the two principal alliances. So fluid is the European scene at this time that it is virtually impossible to forecast the long term outcome. However, one thing is certain—any progress towards a lasting and peaceful settlement must be guided by a very clear understanding of the issues at stake. The dangers inherent in what has now become so politically unstable a situation are all too obvious.

It is against this background that the chapters of this book should be read. Together, they provide an invaluable analysis of the strengths and weaknesses of the Atlantic Alliance, of the state of the United States' economy and the influence it may have upon the courses open, at home and abroad, to the Bush Administration, and of the nature of the tightrope upon which Mikhail Gorbachev must walk as he seeks to progress his plans for *perestroika*.

The quality of the perception shown by my fellow authors reflects the authenticity and validity of their views. The thrust of each chapter and the valuable reminders that all contain of the many factors that must influence the judgements of those whose business it is to look for a way forward and to influence national policy-making, makes their content as relevant today as when they were written.

CHRISTOPHER COKER

December 1989

PART 1

Days of Reckoning?

CHAPTER 1

The United States in Decline?

DAVID GARNHAM

Two countries have dominated international affairs since the Congress of Vienna: Britain (from the Napoleonic era until the First World War) and the United States (since 1945). Like previous hegemons, that is states 'powerful enough to maintain the essential rules governing interstate relations, and willing to do so',[1] these countries used military and economic capabilities to maintain pre-eminence. But the ultimate foundation of national power is economic rather than military, and it is widely acknowledged that Gross National Product (GNP) is the best single measure.[2] Air, naval, and even land forces have become so capital intensive that industrial and technological capacity are essential to the production of military capabilities. GNP also correlates with population size, which reflects the number of potential military recruits, and a nation's capacity (and perhaps willingness) to bear the cost of defence spending.

Given this intimate relationship between economic and military power, America's eroding global economic position during the Reagan years inspired fears of overall American decline. Following the October 1987 Wall Street crash, this issue captured the American imagination. In 1988 historian Paul Kennedy's lengthy study *The Rise and Fall of the Great Powers* remained on *The New York Times* best seller list for thirty-four weeks. This chapter examines three issues: evidence of American decline, interpretations of these data, and their implications for America's ability and willingness to sustain current contributions to Western security.

Evidence of Decline

America has experienced a striking decline in relative economic power since the Second World War. For example, between 1950 and 1987 America's relative share of GNP/GDP among the Group of Seven Western industrial countries (the United States, Japan, West Germany, France, the United Kingdom, Italy and Canada) fell from more than 70 per cent to 43 per cent.[3] Moreover, the rate of decline remained quite constant throughout the period with only rare and brief reversals of the dominant trend.

From 1915 until 1984 foreign assets owned by Americans always exceeded US assets owned by foreigners: this credit balance peaked at $141 billion in 1981. Then, in just five years, America plunged from being the world's principal creditor nation to become the single largest debtor country. In early 1989, America's external debt amounted to approximately $500 billion.[4] Some analysts assert that the Commerce Department's practice of basing asset value on acquisition costs (rather than current market value) exaggerates American indebtedness. Because of inflation, acquisition costs for assets recently acquired by foreigners in America exceed those of older American-owned assets abroad.[5] Other economists contend that official accountings are reasonably accurate considering that nominal assets of American banks due from less developed countries remain overvalued and that official accounts overlook approximately $25 billion in annual net investment by foreigners in the United States.[6] These disputes aside, the salient political reality is that the United States is now a debtor nation, even if it was not in 1986. This represents a profound reversal of America's recent economic position.

Budget deficits have been enormous in recent years, rising from 2.6 per cent of GNP in 1981 to 6.3 per cent in 1983.[7] The deficit declined to 3.8 per cent of GNP in 1988, but it remained larger than those of all other Group of Seven countries excepting only Italy (the United Kingdom even managed a small surplus): Japan (−2.4 per cent), West Germany (−1.7 per cent), France (−1.5 per cent), Britain (+.1 per cent), Canada (−3.1 per cent), and Italy (−11.5 per cent).[8] Moreover, in July 1989, Budget Director Richard Darman predicted a Fiscal Year 1989 deficit of $148 billion, less than five per cent below the previous year's level. Comptroller General Charles A. Bowsher, who heads the General Accounting Office, scorns the legislative-executive agreement which allegedly holds the 1990 budget deficit below $100 billion. If trust fund surpluses such as Social Security are kept separate, as they should be to reflect the need to cover future obligations, then he expects the real deficit to exceed $260 billion. According to Bowsher, 'We are adding $1 trillion every five years to the total deficit, and are digging a huge hole that will be very hard to get out of.[9] One co-sponsor of the Gramm-Rudman-Hollings legislation, Democratic Senator Ernest Hollings, dismissed the $100 billion deficit estimate as a 'fraud.'[10]

These deficits are significant for several reasons. First, they indicate irresponsibility, for Americans are unwilling to reduce government consumption by cutting entitlement programmes or defence spending (which together with interest on the national debt account for most Federal expenditures) or to reduce private consumption through higher taxes. Second, dependence upon foreign loans to finance the deficits undermines America's self-sufficiency. Former Nixon Administration Commerce Secretary Peter Peterson described one way in which American vulnerability is increased. He recalled, the Suez crisis of 1956, when the United States, which held reserves of British sterling as foreigners hold our dollars today, warned the British that we would declare war on the pound if they did not stop their invasion of Egypt. So much for the perils of dependence on foreign investors.[11]

Many economists argue that, 'the best measure of a government's fiscal posture over long periods is whether its debt is rising or falling compared to national income.'[12] In 1980 the accumulated national debt equalled 26 per cent of annual GNP; it surged during the Reagan presidency and equalled 43 per cent of GNP in 1989.[13] In his first presidential speech devoted to economic issues, President Reagan cautioned that,

> Before we reach the day when we can reduce the [Federal] debt ceiling, we may, in spite of our best efforts, see a national debt in excess of a trillion dollars. Now, this is a figure that's literally beyond our comprehension.[14]

But when Reagan retired, the national debt did not total a mere $1,000 billion but exceeded $2,600 billion. Annual interest charges increase by $25 billion each year. At $160 billion (14 per cent of the Federal budget), interest already equals more than one-half the Defense Department budget.

The budget deficits, and the accumulated debt they have spawned, are widely perceived as the most serious problems confronting the country. When asked in November 1988 which of five issues should be the Bush administration's top priority, an overwhelming majority of the American public selected 'reduce the budget deficit.'[15] There is broad agreement that some combination of spending reductions (especially of defence and entitlement programmes which, together with interest payments on the debt, account for nearly 90 per cent of the federal budget) and increased taxes are essential to moderate these deficits. Virtually no one ever believed President Bush's unconditional pledge during the 1988 presidential campaign to reject all increased taxes and modestly to increase military spending.

Former Presidents Jimmy Carter and Gerald Ford co-chaired a prestigious bipartisan commission which developed recommendations to the new President. They explicitly supported a 'freeze in Defense at current levels adjusted for inflation' and also 'non-income tax increases. . . .'[16] Moreover, when chief executive officers of 225 of the largest American corporations were surveyed in December 1988, 68 per cent thought that, 'taxes or user fees should be increased to reduce the budget deficit,' and 62 per cent thought that defence spending should be decreased (compared to 34 per cent who said it should remain constant).[17]

Some conservative economists present a more optimistic analysis, for example Council of Economic Advisers' chairman Michael Boskin. Boskin is best known for developing George Bush's 'flexible freeze' proposal which asserted that the budget deficit could be eliminated in four to five years, without tax increases, simply by limiting the growth of federal spending (not including Social Security and interest on the federal debt) to the inflation rate. Boskin assesses the role of deficits differently depending upon the overall state of the economy. During economic recessions, deficits can provide a desirable stimulus, but 'at full employment,' which the American economy has nearly achieved after six years of sustained economic growth,

> a continuing deficit eventually leads to monetisation of the debt by the Federal Reserve and to acceleration of inflation. This occurs because there is a limit to the amount of government bonds the private sector and the rest of the world are willing to hold.[18]

Therefore, while the short-term effects of deficits do not trouble Boskin greatly, he is concerned by long-term consequences.

Other economists are even more optimistic. The Nobel Laureate Milton Friedman lauds the budget deficits as exerting a positive impact by curtailing the Congress' propensity to increase government spending. He concedes that the budget deficit is a 'hidden tax' and a 'bad tax,' but Friedman concludes that 'it is currently preventing the imposition of a still larger and still worse tax.'[19] This contention prompts some analysts, including Benjamin Friedman, to speculate that the 'hidden agenda' of the Kemp-Roth tax cut 'was deliberately to mortgage the nation's future as a means of forcing Americans to give up government activities which they would otherwise have been able to afford.[20]

Some economists, including Milton Friedman, Robert Heilbroner, and Peter Bernstein,[21] also point out that, even today, the aggregate federal debt equals a smaller proportion of national income that it constituted from 1945 until 1960. But this ignores the fact that recent debt accumulated during years of peace and prosperity. Previously, high levels of American debt as a proportion of national income occurred only during wars or depressions. For example, the federal debt equalled 3 per cent of GNP in 1915 and 27 per cent in 1920, 16 per cent in 1929, 53 per cent in 1940, and 120 per cent in 1945.[22] As Michael Boskin observed, the 1980s were 'the first time we faced sustained large deficits that were not automatically vanishing with an economic recovery.'[23]

Current deficits are structural rather than cyclical. Moreover, interest payments now account for a larger portion of the federal budget than they have since 1948. Henry Kaufman, the influential Wall Street economist, concluded that,

> For the first time since the end of the Second World War, if the economy stalls, the Government will not be able to spend itself out of a recession since the

budget deficit is already at an insupportable magnitude. This is the unfortunate legacy of the budgetary malpractices in this decade.[24]

Federal Reserve Chairman Allen Greenspan has distanced himself from those conservative economists who downplay the deficit's effect. He told the National Economic Commission,

> It is beguiling to contemplate the strong economy of recent years in the context of very large deficits and to conclude that the concerns about the adverse effects of the deficit on the economy have been misplaced. But this argument is fanciful. The deficit has already begun to eat away at the foundations of our economic strength.[25]

Opinions also differ concerning the trade deficit which grew during President Reagan's first seven years in office and peaked at $152 billion in 1987. This deficit diminished to $119 billion in 1988 as the effect of a 50 per cent decline in the dollar's value since 1985 began to take effect. A further small decline was expected during 1989, but the deficit would remain above $110 billion. Meanwhile, the broader current account balance (the balance of payments) deteriorated; this deficit equalled $10 billion a month during the first quarter of 1989.

One frequently mentioned scenario predicts that, eventually, foreigners will refuse to continue such large loans to Americans, and then a substantial trade surplus will be required to repay the accumulated indebtedness. As Michael Boskin wrote,

> each year that we import such large amounts of foreign capital will force us to become a larger and larger net exporter in the future, requiring the pendulum of large trade deficits to large trade surpluses to swing still further.[26]

Many analysts contend that the trade deficit is also structural. C Fred Bergsten contends that,

> no respectable analysis shows the current account deficit, given present policies and exchange rates, ever falling much below $100 billion.[27]

And Henry Kaufman observed that after exports increased 12 per cent in 1987, and 28 per cent in the first seven months of 1988, there was little likelihood of further increases, especially when American industry was already operating at the highest level of capacity in eight years.[28] In 1989, American imports remained high despite evidence of an economic slowdown.

Milton Friedman sees the trade relationship from the other side and advances a more optimistic assessment. He doesn't see the level of capital flowing into the United States as the necessary condition for Americans to continue profligate budget and trade deficits. Instead, Friedman contends that the trade deficit is necessary so that foreigners can accumulate the dollars they are currently investing in the American economy. For Friedman, the driving force is foreigners' desire to invest rather than Americans' desire to consume. Therefore, he asserts that the trade deficit,

> provides the dollars for them to invest and has as its opposite side an equal United States surplus on capital account. There is no way of having the one without the other. . . .[29]

He maintains that the Japanese preference for investing in the United States rather than Japan indicates American strength, not weakness.

The United States is also characterised by an extremely low savings rate. Compared to other NATO countries and Japan, the United States had the third lowest gross annual savings rate for the period 1960–67 (above only Turkey and the United Kingdom), and for 1980–84 the American rate surpassed only Canada, Denmark, and Belgium.[30] During the 1950s, total net savings averaged 6.9 per cent; they equalled 7.5 per cent in the 1960s and 6.1 per cent in the 1970s. Reaganomics predicted a higher savings rate from lower tax rates. Instead, following deep rate cuts, total net savings declined to only 2.9 per cent between 1981 and 1986,[31] and there has been only modest improvement since the low point of 1986 and 1987.

This low savings rate affects investment. For example, the percentage of GNP devoted to investment plus education declined from 26.5 per cent in 1973 to 20.3 per cent in 1987.[32] In 1986, private domestic investment equalled 5.5 per cent of GNP, but nearly 62 per cent was funded by foreign investors because total net savings equalled less than 2 per cent. As Michael Boskin wrote, 'For the first time, in 1986, more of net investment was financed by foreigners than by Americans!'[33]

Given the low rate of investment, it is not surprising that recent evidence appears to confirm the deterioration of America's manufacturing base. Although Commerce Department data seem to indicate that manufacturing's share of GNP has remained constant at 21 to 22 per cent since the Second World War, the department now admits that 'there has probably been some overestimation,'[34] and by one revised estimate, 'manufacturing's share of output declined by three or four percentage points since 1973, most of which occurred between 1979 and 1987.'[35]

There is also deterioration in specific sectors. Services have been one area of perennial trade surpluses; even when other aspects of trade were in deficit, the United States has had a surplus in earnings on foreign investments, airline fares, fees and royalties and other 'invisibles'. However, in the second quarter of 1988, and as a direct consequence of the United States now being a debtor rather than a creditor country, the services sector was in deficit for the first time in thirty years.

Americans have been particularly proud and confident of their technological superiority, but in 1986 and 1987 the country imported more high technology goods than were exported. Moreover, the United States' share of global electronics production (including computers, telecommunications, and consumer electronics) declined from over 50 per cent in 1984 to less than 40 per cent in 1987.[36] In 1988, Japan surpassed American production of sophisticated machinery to etch electronic circuits on to silicon. Even America's supercomputing lead is under siege from Japanese competitors and, in early 1989, a presidential advisory committee warned that the United States might fall behind Japan in applying new technologies for high-temperature superconductors.[37] These developments caused considerable consternation in the Pentagon, and in 1988 a study group of the Defense Science Board, distressed by 'an increasing loss of technological leadership to both our allies and adversaries,' recommended a larger Defense Department role in setting national economic policy.[38] In 1989, another Pentagon study concluded that of twenty-two technologies considered crucial to United States security, Japan had a significant lead in six fields (and the Soviets in two others).[39] American competitiveness is also reduced by the fact that civilian research and development constitutes only 1.8 per cent of GNP in the United States compared to 2.6 per cent in the Federal Republic and 2.8 per cent in Japan.[40] American competitiveness is hobbled because so much of the research budget is allocated to military rather than civilian projects.

Is This Decline?

America's relative decline is clear, not only since 1950 but in some respects even when compared with the 1970s. But it is also clear that the United States retains the largest national economy (roughly two-thirds larger than Japan's and five times larger than Germany's). These two facts leave substantial room to dispute whether the decline involves the end of hegemony, or a less profound alteration which leaves the basic structure intact.

Paul Kennedy's well-publicised formulation describes the United States as the latest victim (following the Habsburgs, Napoleonic France, and Britain) of 'imperial overstretch,' the propensity of 'Great Powers in relative decline' [to] instinctively respond by spending more on 'security,' and thereby divert potential resources from 'investment' and compound their long-term dilemma.[41] According to Robert Gilpin's more comprehensive theory of hegemonic decline, hegemons are undone by both internal and external factors. Internally, expenditures for defence and consumption crowd out investment; externally, the costs of leadership become increasingly onerous, and, as time passes, hegemons lose the

technological edge upon which their pre-eminence was initially established.[42] The previous section presented numerous examples of how these
processes have affected the United States.

Gilpin reckons that American hegemony ended in October 1979 with
Bonn's refusal to support the dollar. This forced the Carter Administration
to implement a restrictive monetary policy.

> 'This was,' Gilpin writes, 'the first time in the postwar era that the United
> States made a major change in its domestic economic policy in response to
> foreign pressure'.[43]

Henry Kaufman agrees that,

> the United States is no longer the world's pre-eminent economic power, and
> the trend is toward sharing power with its trading partners.[44]

The economist Mancur Olson presents a very different explanation of
American decline. Olson's analysis is complex and not easily summarised,
but its essence is that efficiencies and rigidities tend to afflict stable societies
which go long periods without social upheavals. With the passage of time,
'distributional coalitions,' i.e. special interest groups such as professional
associations, trade unions, trade associations, and cartels accrete in such
countries. Their effect is to diminish economic efficiency and increase
political divisions. They also retard the decision-making process, so that

> distributional coalitions slow down a society's capacity to adopt new tech-
> nologies and to reallocate resources in response to changing conditions, and
> thereby reduce the rate of economic growth.[45]

Social upheavals such as military occupations and revolutions are effica-
cious, for they sweep away the accumulated interest groups which erode a
society's efficiency. Olson believes this explains Japan and West Germany's
rapid economic growth since 1945, for

> it follows that countries whose distributional coalitions have been emasculated
> or abolished by totalitarian governments or foreign occupation should grow
> relatively quickly after a free and stable legal order is established.[46]

Conversely, countries such as Britain and the United States,

> that have had democratic freedom of organisation without upheaval or in-
> vasion the longest will suffer the most from growth-repressing organisations
> and combinations.[47]

Quite a large literature now exists to challenge these scenarios of
American decline. One frequent criticism of the Gilpin/Kennedy thesis is

that current American military expenditures (approximately 6 per cent of GNP) actually constitute a share of GNP only two-thirds as large as during the 1950s and 1960s.[48] This is cited as evidence that no simple relationship connects defence expenditures and economic growth, for the American economy thrived in the earlier period when the proportional level of military spending was substantially higher. Walt Rostow made a parallel argument in writing that Taiwan and South Korea, with 'a proportionate military outlay higher than the United States, [enjoy] a *per capita* rate of growth almost four times higher.'[49]

Actually, these countries allocate approximately the same percentage of GNP to defence as the United States, not more, as Rostow contends.[50] There are, moreover, substantial differences between the three economies which preclude facile comparisons. For example, while defence expenditures equal 27 per cent of American central governmental expenditures, the comparable figure is one-third in South Korea and one-half in Taiwan. According to Gilpin, national income can be divided into three parts: defence, consumption, and productive investment. The United States has a more extensive social welfare programme than the Newly Industrialised Countries (NICs), so more is consumed leaving fewer resources available for defence or investment. Even more significantly, Taiwan has 'the highest savings rate and the largest foreign reserve (on a *per capita* basis) in the world . . . a savings rate that never fell below 25 per cent of gross domestic product since 1970—and was as high as 34.9 per cent at one time. . . .'[51] This also moderates the negative economic effect of high levels of defence spending. Nonetheless, despite a much higher savings rate, and less competition from other government expenditures, there is evidence that military spending does hamper the Taiwanese economy.[52]

Other critics argue that although the United States' position has declined substantially from its apogee in the period 1945–50, the decline during the last two decades is modest or nonexistent.[53] A related argument emphasises that the United States retains very substantial 'structural power' defined as,

> the power to choose and to shape the structures of the global economy within which other states, their political institutions, their economic enterprises, and (not least) their professional people have to operate.[54]

Susan Strange sees evidence of America's structural power in several contexts. In the security arena, Western Europe and Japan remain dependent upon American conventional and nuclear deterrence. Concerning the global production system, nearly one-half of the 300 largest firms were United States-based, meaning that

> the decision-making power over the world's production structure still lies, not in Europe or Japan, but in the United States.[55]

America also dominates international finance, for

> to run a persistent [balance-of-payments] deficit for a quarter of a century with impunity indicates not American weakness, but rather American power in the system.[56]

And finally,

> America continued to dominate the world's knowledge structure. . . . Overall, the United States still leads in the advanced technology sectors.[57]

Until quite recently, each of the assertions was manifestly true; as I have previously indicated, it is less clear that they remain true today. One additional dimension deserves mention. *Business Week* publishes an annual listing of the 1,000 largest global corporations ranked by market value. The periodical declares that,

> Market value is the best way to rank corporations . . . because it's the true bottom line: It's what the free market system determines a company is worth.[58]

According to the 1989 ranking, 353 of the 1,000 largest firms are American, and 345 are Japanese, but 53 of the top 100 firms are Japanese compared to 35 American, and the five largest firms are all Japanese. The market value of the single largest firm, Nippon Telegraph and Telephone ($164 billion) exceeded the combined market value of the three largest American corporations (IBM, Exxon, and General Electric). Moreover, 47 per cent of the aggregate market value of these 1,000 firms was Japanese ($2,999 billion), and only 32 per cent was American ($2,069 billion), followed by the United Kingdom ($451 billion), and West Germany ($151 billion). It is true, however, that American firms remain more profitable; eleven of the fifteen most profitable firms were American, and only one (Toyota) was Japanese.[59]

No one disputes that the United States remains a very powerful economic actor, but the underpinnings of American power have atrophied. Nixon could close the gold window, as Strange observed, but Carter could not force Bonn to inflate, and the health of the American economy now depends on massive foreign purchases of government debt.

Implications for Burden Sharing

All agree that the United States possesses less relative power than forty years ago; the disagreement concerns the magnitude of America's relative decline in recent decades. Moreover, the margin of power which hegemons require is also ambiguous. According to Samuel Huntington:

if 'hegemony' means having 40 per cent or more of world economic activity (a percentage Britain never remotely approximated during its hegemonic years), American hegemony disappeared long ago. If hegemony means producing 20 to 25 per cent of the world product and twice as much as any other individual country, American hegemony looks quite secure.[60]

Actually, even today the American economy is not twice as large as Japan's. It is true that some indicators suggest that the rate of American decline slowed after the early post-war years, for example America's share of the global product. But other measures indicate a continuing or even an accelerating decline, for example the American proportion of the aggregate product of the Group of Seven, the balance of foreign indebtedness, and the weakened technological base. Unfortunately, the allocation of burdens within the Western Alliance failed to adjust to these new realities.

NATO estimated that in 1988 the United States allocated 6.1 per cent of GDP to defence while the NATO-European countries averaged 3.3 per cent.[61] Meanwhile, Japan's defence expenditures have barely crept above the 1 per cent level. A generation ago, there were sound reasons why the United States should devote a significantly larger proportion of its resources to military spending than its allies. But now, considering the equal affluence of Japan, the United States, and the principal Western European allies, these conditions have evaporated. In 1987 American GDP *per capita* ($13,564) exceeded the NATO average ($11,278) by only 20 per cent and was actually *below* the level of Norway ($17,024), Denmark ($15,047), Luxembourg ($14,978), and the Federal Republic ($14,701) and approximately equivalent to France ($13,363). Yet, all these countries devoted substantially lower percentages of GDP to defence than did the United States: Norway (3.3), Denmark (2.2), Luxembourg (1.3), the Federal Republic (3.0) and France (3.8).[62]

This situation is inequitable, and America's economic problems make it unsustainable. Consequently, the burden-sharing issue is receiving renewed attention, especially from the Congress. A notable recent example is the report of the Defence Burdensharing Panel of the House Committee on Armed Services.[63] The following are among the Panel's more provocative statements:

- Many Americans feel that we are competing 100 per cent militarily with the Soviets and 100 per cent economically with our defence allies. Some have said that the United States has incurred all the burdens of empire and few, if any, of the benefits.[64]
- The Panel believes that if the United States is spending more on defence than the combined total of the rest of the allies in order to be the 'boss,' the United States is not getting its money's worth.[65]
- Our allies are not sufficiently aware of the strong political pressure in this country to reduce our defence commitments to our allies

unless they are willing to shoulder more of the burden. This view is shared by the Congress.[66]

Senator Bennett Johnston (D-La), who sought unsuccessfully to succeed Senator Byrd as Majority Leader in the 101st Congress, went further; he described the current situation as 'astonishingly unfair'. And Chairman Sam Nunn of the Senate Armed Services Committee, the most influential member of the Congress on these issues, wrote that

> despite the shift in relative economic power to our allies, the cost of defence has remained disproportionately on American shoulders. Adjustments are long overdue.[67]

Initiatives have emerged more slowly from the executive branch, but they are potentially more significant. At the end of 1988, the Secretaries of State and Defense issued a report expressing their conviction that,

> a more equitable sharing of the roles, risks and responsibilities for the common defence is needed and is achievable.[68]

Meanwhile, during the previous year Deputy Defense Secretary William Howard Taft IV had reviewed this issue with the Western Europeans, Japan, and Korea. Taft told the French in July 1988, that

> without a European effort it would be more and more difficult to make military expenditures in Europe politically acceptable in the United States.[69]

Moreover, the US Army has pondered the option of six month tours for European battalions rather than the present policy of permanent deployments. There are 200,000 family members in Europe, so troop costs would be significantly reduced, by perhaps $2 billion annually, if dependants remained in the United States. There is, reportedly, stiff opposition to this plan within the Army, at least in part because it could be the first step toward removing American troops from the continent.[70] However, the Bush Administration will withdraw and demobilise 4,000 US Army soldiers that had controlled the Pershing 2 and ground-launched cruise missiles in the Federal Republic. Furthermore, NATO's proposal at the Vienna talks on Conventional Armed Forces in Europe (CFE) could produce larger reductions. Approximately 30,000 troops would be withdrawn to satisfy the ceiling of 275,000 Soviet and American air and ground forces outside of national territory within the Atlantic to Ural zone.

The burden-sharing issue is complex, and this chapter does not attempt a detailed examination. It is pertinent, however, to note that both Americans and Europeans have produced a series of studies to publicise Europe's contribution. A recent example is the Eurogroup's May 1988 report *Western Defence: the European Role in Nato.*[71] An important American example is the Secretary of Defense's annual *Report on Allied Contributions to the Common Defense.* Although the legislation mandating this report was motivated by Congressional concern that the Allies were shirking their responsibilities, the report itself portrays allied efforts as favourably as possible. Former Reagan Administration Assistant Secretary of Defense Richard Perle told the Defense Burdensharing Panel,

> The exercise in preparing the Annual Report on Burdensharing is largely an exercise in thinking of ways to put the best possible gloss on some pretty dismal figures. I know it because I superintended it for a while—and we look for statistics that make the allies look good.[72]

Americans are no longer wealthier than their allies, and they are slipping behind in the international economic competition. In these circumstances, Americans usually emphasise measures such as the percentage of GNP devoted to military spending, and defence expenditures *per capita*, which show the United States bearing an inordinate share of the burden. Europeans argue that their level of military spending grew more rapidly than American defence spending during the 1970s and 1980s, but Defense Secretary Cheney reported that between 1971 and 1987 non-United States NATO spending grew only slightly more: 32 per cent compared to 25 per cent for the United States.[73] Moreover, the level of European spending was and remains substantially lower.

It is true that the European Allies provide 90 per cent of the manpower, 80 per cent of the tanks, and 80 per cent of the combat aircraft for *peacetime* forces in Europe. Nonetheless, Americans continue to spend more to defend Europe than Europeans spend to defend themselves. Studies by the United States Department of Defense and the General Accounting Office estimate that more than 55 per cent of the US defence budget goes to defend Western Europe.[74] This means that American *per capita* expenditures for Western Europe defence exceed those of most European nations. In 1988, total American defence expenditures equalled $820 *per capita.*[75] or approximately $451 *per capita* (55 per cent of $820) for Western European defence. Only three European countries exceeded America's *per capita* level of expenditure for European defence; they were Britain ($502), France ($529), and Norway ($529); most European-NATO members spent substantially less. These comparisons become increasingly salient as the deficits and the accumulated debt depress American defence spending.

During President Reagan's first term, inflation-adjusted defence spending rose by 50 per cent. In the early 1980s, there was a popular mandate for higher military spending because a majority of Americans believed that the Soviet Union had equalled or surpassed the military capability of the

United States. In 1980, 60 per cent of the public believed that military spending was 'too little,' and only 12 per cent considered it 'too much'. By 1985, only 15 per cent considered it 'too little' while 42 per cent considered it 'too much'.[76] Support for military spending gradually evaporated during the 1980s, the victim of much higher levels of defence expenditures, revelations of Soviet deficiencies which *glasnost* unveiled, and Mikhail Gorbachev's less threatening policies. There is also a widespread perception that a significant portion of President Reagan's defence build-up was squandered. For example, in a February 1988 national survey 68 per cent of respondents said there was 'a lot' of 'waste, fraud, and inefficiency' in defence spending; 29 per cent thought there was 'some,' and 2 per cent said 'not very much.'[77] Even Reagan Administration Assistant Defense Secretary Lawrence Korb confirmed that, 'no overall strategy guided the defense buildup. . . . Weinberger was simply throwing money at the problem, and allowing the Services to set priorities.'[78]

Given the budget deficit, a lower perception of Soviet threat, and perceived Pentagon waste and corruption, military spending will continue to decline. As Chairman Les Aspin of the House Armed Services Committee observed, the factor most likely to push up defence spending is 'Soviet adventurism' and the factor most likely to depress defence spending is the 'continuing massive trade and fiscal deficits.' In 'an era of Gorbachev, *glasnost*, and *perestroika*,' Soviet adventurism is clearly less likely than 'persistent US deficits in an era of no tax increases and more non-military budget cuts.' Consequently, Aspin predicted that

> zero real growth . . . is the very best that the Pentagon can hope for. What's more likely is more of the negative real growth that there's been in the last four defence budgets.[79]

Some influential advice goes much further. Henry Kaufman advocated reducing military spending from 6.1 per cent of GNP to 4 per cent.[80] This would be the lowest level in the post-war era, even below the Carter Administration level when DoD spending dipped to 5.1 per cent of GNP during Fiscal Years 1978 and 1979.

Retrenchment is complicated by a five-year Department of Defense (DoD) budget which assumes 2 per cent annual real growth. As former Defense Secretary James Schlesinger observed, this means 'We are going to have to reduce the force structure.'[81] It will be necessary to cut the number of divisions, naval forces, and/or air forces. Indeed, even the principal proponent of a 600 ship navy, former Navy Secretary John Lehman, now believes the naval mission could be sustained with 13 carrier battle groups (rather than the goal of 15) if European allies and Japan did more to help defend Persian Gulf oilfields.[82]

The necessity for force reductions is aggravated by the fact that DoD expends only half its budget during the year when it is appropriated:

military pay and operating funds are spent quickly; research and development funds are spent more slowly, and less than 15 per cent of procurement and military construction funds are spent during the first year. Consequently, cutting procurement funding is not an effective way to reduce the deficit. Chairman Aspin estimates that one must

> cut about seven bucks out of the procurement budget to save a dollar of Outlays. To make real progress, he [the President] would have to cut the fast spenders, such as the military personnel and operating accounts. But cutting there means cutting out people and readiness, and thus immediate military strength ... to cut the deficit he needs to cut outlays, but to cut outlays he needs to cut the wrong things.[83]

America's relative decline has dramatised the connections among economic, political, and military power. Until very recently, American national security officials emphasised diplomatic and military agendas while largely ignoring the economic basis of national power. This is changing. Former Secretaries of State Henry Kissinger and Cyrus Vance recently wrote that,

> America's role in the world has become directly dependent on the strength and performance of the US economy. ... When we served as Secretaries of State, only a relatively small portion of our time was spent on international economic issues. Our successors do not have this luxury.[84]

This chapter has addressed the relationships between America's relative economic decline, lowered levels of military spending, and Alliance burden-sharing. The system of Western security, and the division of burdens among the participating states, were established long ago at the acme of United States' power. Much has changed in forty years, and as Kissinger has stated,

> we are still the strongest nation in the world, but we can no longer guarantee the balance of power alone.[85]

The diminution of America's economic power is forcing a reduction of military spending which accentuates the burden-sharing controversy. Fortunately, America has declined in relation to her allies rather than the Soviet Union. This should facilitate the creation of a less centralised Western security system with greater congruence between the allocation of burdens and current economic realities.

Notes

1. Robert O Keohane and Joseph S Nye, Jr *Power and Inter-dependence*. Boston: Little, Brown, 1977, p. 44.
2. See Robert Gilpin *The Political Economy of International Relations*. Princeton: Princeton

University Press, 1987, p. 76; Robert O Keohane *After Hegemony: Cooperation and Discord in the World Political Economy.* Princeton: Princeton University Press, 1984, p. 32; and A F K Organski and Jacek Kugler *The War Ledger.* Chicago: University of Chicago Press, 1980, pp. 33–38.

3. See Mark E Rupert and David P Rapkin 'The Erosion of U.S. Leadership Capabilities,' in Paul M Johnson and William R Thompson, eds., *Rhythms in Politics and Economics.* New York: Praeger, 1985, p. 163 and Central Intelligence Agency *The World Factbook 1988.* Washington, DC: US Government Printing Office, 1988.

4. See Clyde H Farnsworth, 'Money Loss Grows for Poorer Lands, World Bank Finds,' *The New York Times,* 19 December 1988, p. 1.

5. One Rand Corporation study calculated a discrepancy at the end of 1986 between a nominal American indebtedness of $264 billion and an actual American credit balance of $50 billion. See David Binder and Clyde H Farnsworth 'Pauper or Prince?' *The New York Times,* 25 October 1988, p. 12.

6. See Benjamin M Friedman *Day of Reckoning: The Consequences of American Economic Policy Under Reagan and After.* New York: Random House, 1988, pp. 229–230.

7. Martin Tolchin 'Paradox of Reagan Budgets Hints Contradiction in Legacy,' *The New York Times,* February 16, 1988, p. 12.

8. Source: 'Le tableau de bord de l'économie du groupe des Sept,' *Le Monde,* 4 February 1989, p. 23.

9. Nathaniel C Nash 'No. 1 Whistle Blower Derides Deficit Figures,' *The New York Times,* 24 April 1989, p. 10.

10. See 'So Why Ain't It Dead,' *Barron's,* 10 July 1989, p. 20.

11 Peter G. Peterson 'The Morning After,' *The Atlantic Monthly,* Vol. 260, No. 4 (October 1987), p. 54.

12. Benjamin M Friedman *Day of Reckoning: The Consequences of American Economic Policy Under Reagan and After.* New York: Random House, 1988, pp. 88–89.

13. Friedman *Day of Reckoning,* p. 115 and Christopher Lehmann-Haupt, 'What's Right With the National Debt,' *The New York Times,* 27 July 1989, p. 14.

14. Quoted in John M Berry 'The Legacy of Reaganomics,' *The Washington Post National Weekly Edition,* 19–25 December 1988, p. 6.

15. Respondents were asked to, 'Pick the issue that should be the Bush administration's top priority'. The choices and percentages were: reduce the deficit (44 per cent); protect American jobs from foreign competition (20 per cent); strengthen programmes that help families (15 per cent); negotiate further arms reductions with the USSR (12 per cent); and improve protection of the environment (8 per cent). Source: Times Mirror Survey of 2,022 voters conducted 9 November by The Gallup Organization. *The New York Times,* 18 December 1988, p. E23.

16. Gerald Ford, Jimmy Carter, *et al. America Agenda: Report to the Forty-First President of the United States* (America Agenda, 1988), Part II, pp. 8–9. For similar recommendations, see C Fred Bergsten, *America in the World Economy.* Washington, DC: Institute for International Economics, 1988; Friedman, *Day of Reckoning;* Henry Kaufman 'Memo to the Next President,' *New York Times Magazine,* 9 October 1988, pp. 32–40 and p. 53; and Peterson 'The Morning After.'

17. Source: David Kirkpatrick 'CEOs to Bush: Raise Taxes Now,' *Fortune,* 16 January 1989, pp. 95–96; N equalled 225 CEOs of Fortune 500 and Service 500 companies. The survey was conducted 5–15 December 1988.

18. Michael J Boskin *Reagan and the Economy: The Successes, Failures and Unfinished Agenda.* San Francisco: Institute for Contemporary Studies, 1987, p. 1971.

19. Milton Friedman 'Why the Twin Deficits Are a Blessing,' *The Wall Street Journal,* 14 December 1988, p. A14.

20. Friedman *Day of Reckoning,* p. 23. Senator Daniel Patrick Moynihan (D-NY) interprets a speech by President Reagan barely two weeks following his inauguration in 1981 as foreshadowing this goal of raising deficits sufficiently high to curtail government spending. See E J Dionne, Jr 'Reagan Debt Legacy: His Trap for Democrats,' *The New York Times,* 2 December 1988, p. 11. This effect is also applauded by Robert E Hall 'Are Deficits Sinking the Economy?' *The New York Times,* 21 December 1988, p. 27.

21. See Robert Heilbroner and Peter Bernstein *The Debt and the Deficit: False Alarms/Real Possibilities.* New York: W W Norton, 1989.

22. See Gary M Anderson, 'US Federal Deficits and the National Debt: A Political and Economic History,' in James M Buchanan, *et al.*, eds., *Deficits*. New York: Basil Blackwell, 1986, p. 14.

23. Boskin *Reagan and the Economy*, p. 174.

24. Kaufman 'Memo to the Next President,' pp. 36–38.

25. Quoted in Peter T. Kilborn 'US Budget Deficit Must Be Cut Soon, Greenspan Warns,' *The New York Times*, 17 November 1988, p. 10. Greenspan's predecessor at the Federal Reserve, Paul Volker, expressed similar views. See Peter T Kilborn 'Volker Warns Deficit Perils Stock and Currency Markets,' *The New York Times*, 1 December 1988, p. 1 and p. 13.

26. Boskin *Reagan and the Economy*, p. 189.

27. Bergsten *America in the World Economy*, p. 4

28. See Kaufman 'Memo to the Next President,' p. 34 and p. 38.

29. Friedman 'Why the Twin Deficits Are a Blessing,' p. A14.

30. Calculated from data in Leonard Sullivan, Jr and Jack A LeCuyer *Comprehensive Security and Western Prosperity*. Lanham, MD: University Press of America, 1988, p. 143.

31. Calculated from data in Boskin *Reagan and the Economy*, p. 186.

32. See Herbert Stein 'For Growth, Cut Butter Not Guns,' *The New York Times*, 6 December 1988, p. 27.

33. Boskin *Reagan and the Economy*, p. 188.

34. This also raises questions concerning increases in manufacturing productivity which is measured using manufacturing output. It is likely that productivity increases in the 1980s would place the US near the bottom among the Group of Seven rather than in the middle as previously estimated. See Louis Uchitelle 'Strength in Manufacturing Overstated by Faulty Data,' *The New York Times*, 28 November 1988, p. 21 and p. 31.

35. Lawrence Mishel 'Of Manufacturing's Mismeasurement,' *The New York Times*, 27 November 1988, p. F3.

36. Lawrence M Fisher 'US Share Declines in Electronics,' *The New York Times*, 5 January 1989, p. 23.

37. See David E Sanger 'A High-Tech Lead in Danger,' *The New York Times*, 18 December 1988, p. F1 and p. F6 and Andrew Pollack 'Bringing Superconductivity Down to Earth,' *The New York Times*, 8 January 1989, p. E6.

38. John H Cushman Jr. 'Pentagon Is Urged to Be More Active in Economic Policy,' *The New York Times*, 19 October 1988, p. 1 and p. 45.

39. See Martin Tolchin 'Technology Report Finds Japan Leads in 6 Areas,' *The New York Times*, 16 May 1989, p. 39. Japan led in: microelectronics, compound semiconductors, integrated optics, robotics, superconductivity, and biotechnology materials and processing; the Soviets led in high-powered microwaves and pulsed power lasers.

40. See 'America and Research Roulette,' *The New York Times*, 6 December 1988, p. 26.

41. Paul Kennedy *The Rise and Fall of the Great Powers: Economic Change and Military Conflict from 1500 to 2000*. New York: Random House, 1987, p. xxiii.

42. See Robert Gilpin *War and Change in World Politics*. New York: Cambridge University Press, 1981, pp. 156–185.

43. Gilpin *The Political Economy of International Relations*, p. 332.

44. Kaufman 'Memo to the President,' p. 40. For related arguments see David P Calleo *Beyond American Hegemony: The Future of the Western Alliance*. New York: Basic Books, 1987; David P Calleo, Harold van B Cleveland, and Leonard Silk, 'The Dollar and the Defense of the West,' *Foreign Affairs*, Vol. 66, No. 4 (Spring 1988), pp. 846–862; and Walter Russell Mead *Mortal Splendor: The American Empire in Transition*. Boston: Houghton Mifflin, 1987, pp. 213–276.

45. Mancur Olson *The Rise and Decline of Nations: Economic Growth, Stagflation, and Social Rigidities*. New Haven: Yale University Press, 1982, p. 65. For a critique of Olson's theory, see David R. Cameron 'Distributional Coalitions and Other Sources of Economic Stagnation: On Olson's *Rise and Decline of Nations*, *International Organization*, Vol. 42, No. 4 (Autumn 1988), pp. 561–603.

46. Olson *The Rise and Decline of Nations*, p. 75.

47. Olson *The Rise and Decline of Nations*, p. 77. Actually, Olson pulls his punches with respect to the US, writing that, 'it is hard to say exactly what growth performance the theory offered here would predict for the United States. . . .' (p. 94).

48. See, for example, Herbert Stein 'Cutting the Lean out of Defense,' *The Wall Street Journal*, 17 February 1985, also published as *Defense and the Deficit* (Washington, DC: Committee on the Present Danger, 8 March 1985), and Murray Weidenbaum 'Why Defense Spending Doesn't Matter,' *The National Interest*, No. 16 (Summer 1989), pp. 91–96.

49. W W Rostow 'Beware of Historians Bearing False Analogies,' *Foreign Affairs*, Vol. 66, No. 4 (Spring 1988), p. 866.

50. See Central Intelligence Agency *The World Factbook 1988*. Washington, DC: US Government Printing Office, 1988.

51. Steve Chan 'Defense Burden and Economic Growth: Unravelling the Taiwanese Enigma,' *American Political Science Review*, Vol. 82, No. 3 (September 1988), p. 917.

52. See Chan 'Defense Burden and Economic Growth,' p. 916.

53. See Samuel P Huntington 'The US—Decline or Renewal?' *Foreign Affairs*, Vol. 67, No. 2 (Winter 1988/89), p. 82; Joseph S Nye, Jr. 'Understanding US strength,' *Foreign Policy*, No. 72 (Fall 1988), pp. 105–108; and Bruce M Russett 'The Mysterious Case of Vanishing Hegemony; Or, Is Mark Twain Really Dead?' *International Organization*, Vol. 39, No. 2 (Spring 1985), p. 231.

54. Susan Strange 'The Persistent Myth of Lost Hegemony,' *International Organization*, Vol. 41, No. 4 (Autumn 1987), p. 565; also see Susan Strange *Casino Capitalism*. London: Blackwell, 1986, pp. 22–23.

55. Strange 'The Persistent Myth of Lost Hegemony,' p. 568.

56. Strange 'The Persistent Myth of Lost Hegemony,' p. 569.

57. Strange 'The Persistent Myth of Lost Hegemony,' pp. 569–570.

58. 'The Global 1000,' *Business Week*, 18 July 1988, p. 137.

59. See 'The Global 1000,' *Business Week*, 17 July 1989, pp. 139–144. Based on market capitalisation on 31 May 1989.

60. Huntington 'The US—Decline or Renewal?,' p. 84. Bruce Russett points out that, 'the United Kingdom was never, even at its peak in the nineteenth century, the dominant power as measured by either GNP or military expenditures.' Russett 'The Mysterious Case of Vanishing Hegemony,' p. 211; also see p. 212. However, Britain was the principal manufacturing nation for several decades in the late nineteenth century; see Aaron L Friedberg *The Weary Titan: Britain and the Experience of Relative Decline, 1895–1905*. Princeton: Princeton University Press, 1988, p. 26 and Kennedy *The Rise and Fall of the Great Powers*, p. 149.

61. See NATO Press Service, *Financial and Economic Data Relating to NATO Defence*, M-DPC-2(88)74 (Brussels: NATO, 1 December 1988), p. 4.

62. See NATO, *Financial and Economic Data*, p. 5 and p. 4.

63. Defense Burdensharing Panel, *Report of the Defense Burdensharing Panel* (Washington, DC: Committee on Armed Services, US House of Representatives, August 1988).

64. *Report of the Defense Burdensharing Panel*, p. 12. For example, a February 1988 survey of 1,000 registered voters by the Daniel Yankelovich Group found that, 'Six in 10 said they believe that "the expense of defending so many countries is a serious threat to our national security," and 8 in 10 "strongly" or "somewhat" agree that we "cannot afford to defend so many nations". . . . 6 in 10 "strongly agree" (and 8 in 10 "strongly" to "somewhat" agree) that "economic is as important as military power" in today's world.' Jack Beatty ' "Burden-Sharing," Jolted,' *The New York Times*, 3 April 1988.

65. *Report of the Defense Burdensharing Panel*, p. 45.

66. *Report of the Defense Burdensharing Panel*, p. 61.

67. Sam Nunn 'Our Allies Have to Do More,' *The New York Times*, 10 July 1988, p. 31.

68. Quoted in Richard Halloran 'US Report Prods the Allies To Increase Military Outlays,' *The New York Times*, 29 December 1988, p. 7.

69. Quoted in 'Le secrétaire adjoint américain à la défense appelle les Européens à un effort budgétaire,' *Le Monde*, 22 July 1988, p. 4.

70. See Richard Halloran 'Army Weighs Shorter Troop Tours,' *The New York Times*, 18 December 1988, p. 18.

71. Eurogroup *Western Defense: the European Role in NATO*. Brussels: The Eurogroup, May 1988. Also see Government of the Federal Republic of Germany *The German Contribution to the Common Defense*. Bonn: Press and Information Offices of the Federal Repub-

lic of Germany and the Federal Ministry of Defense, 1986; Defence Planning Committee *Enhancing Alliance Collective Security: Shared Roles, Risks, and Responsibilities in the Alliance*. Brussels: NATO, December 1988; British Information Services, *Burdensharing, Defence Trade and Alliance Relationships: The United Kingdom View* (31 May 1988); and Michael Legge 'The View From London,' *The National Interest*, Number 12 (Summer 1988), pp. 34–42.

72. *Report of the Defense Burdensharing Panel*, p. 30. Also see Gordon Adams and Eric Munz *Fair Shares: Bearing the Burden of the NATO Alliance*. Washington, DC: Defense Budget Project, March 1988.

73. Source: Richard B Cheney *Report on Allied Contributions to the Common Defense: A Report to the United States Congress by the Secretary of Defense*. Washington, DC: US Department of Defense, April 1989, p. 95.

74. See Richard Halloran 'Two Studies Say Defense of Western Europe is Biggest US Military Cost,' *The New York Times*, 20 July 1984, p. 2.

75. See NATO *Financial and Economic Data*, p. 3.

76. See Ted Goertzel 'Public Opinion Concerning Military Spending in the United States: 1937–1985,' *Journal of Political and Military Sociology*, Vol. 15, No. 1. (Spring 1987), p. 63.

77. The survey for the Americans Talk Security Project was conducted February 17–24, 1988 by the Daniel Yankelovich Group. The sample equalled 1,004 registered voters.

78. Lawrence J Korb 'Spending Without Strategy: The FY 1988 Annual Defense Department Report,' *International Security*, Vol. 12, No. 1 (Summer 1987), p. 169.

79. Congressman Les Aspin 'What the Next President Should Know About National Defense,' Remarks to Science Applications International Corporation, La Jolla, CA, 8 December 1988, pp. 7–8.

80. See Kaufman 'Memo to the Next President,' p. 36.

81. Quoted in Wilson 'Not Enough Bang for the Buck,' p. 38.

82. See John H Cushman, Jr 'Ex-Insider Who Elects To Remain on Outside,' *The New York Times*, 6 January 1989, p. 11.

83. Aspin 'What the Next President Should Know,' p. 9.

84. Henry Kissinger and Cyrus Vance 'Bipartisan Objectives for American Foreign Policy,' *Foreign Affairs*, Vol. 66, No. 5 (Summer 1988), p. 910.

85. Quoted in Bruno Dethomas 'Prospérité économique sur fond de déclin,' *Le Monde*, 3 November 1988, p. 7.

CHAPTER 2

Intimations of Mortality?

CHRISTOPHER COKER

'Let us remember that we shall . . . fall into the decline and infirmities of old age' (John Quincy Adams 1787)

'It is a bleak moment when the heralds proclaim the passing of the dead, and the great officers of state break their staves. But is sadder still when it is the victim's own voice that announces his decadence, when it is the victim's own hand that breaks the staff. . .' (Lord Rosebery's comment on Lord Randolph Churchill in Philip Guedalla *A Gallery* 1926)

According to some writers, the United States has been in decline for much longer than even the most pessimistic analysts would contend. In 1942 Joseph Schumpeter predicted that America's entrepreneurship would be destroyed by mechanisation, which would in turn rob businessmen of their spirit of adventure and deprive the economy of dynamic management. His *cri de cœur* about the passing of America's entrepreneurial vitality on the eve of its rise as a superpower bears a striking similarity to Arnold Toynbee's theory that Rome's decline could be traced to the Second Punic War, which destroyed the political ecology of the Italian peninsula, and thus the base of the Roman Empire whose decline and eventual fall six centuries later were to be captured so vividly by Edward Gibbon.[1]

Twenty-five years later, the pessimists were dealing a stronger suit. Had the American century come to an end? One writer felt that the century had passed in the closing days of the Second World War, that the United States had lost its status as a superpower by the late 1960s, that America's history 'as a nation [was] coming to an end'.[2] Writing a few years earlier, Ronald Steele contended that the curtain had run down on the *Pax Americana* faster than it had on the *Pax Britannica*, which had been relegated to the scrapheap of history within twenty-five years of the fall of Singapore (1942).[3]

In the mid-1960s, as the United States found itself mired in the Vietnam War, Donald Brandon concluded a book on his country's foreign policy with the plea that 'America must come of age', that it must escape its political adolescence if it was ever to reach maturity.[4] By 1973, it seemed too late. As the Vietnam War came to an ignominious end, the noted political columnist Henry Brandon confidently wrote of 'The Retreat of American Power', claiming that its 'design' had already been delineated. Only its pace and extent remained a matter of speculation.[5] Throughout the early 1970s, the American public may have been bewildered and bedazzled at turns by the artful statecraft of the master illusionist Henry Kissinger, whose brilliant diplomatic *tromps l'œil* seemed to compensate for any loss of power the United States had incurred in Indo-China. Yet it was Kissinger, the ultimate apologist of Bismarckian politics, who defined diplomacy in the same period as the 'art of restraining the exercise of power',[6] conscious of how little real power the United States enjoyed.

In addressing the whole subject, it is not clear whether the peddlers of doom are talking about national decadence, imperial retreat, or the passing of an era—the American century—a historical concept first propagated in 1942 by the writer Henry Luce. In such circumstances, it is hardly surprising that modern scholars should have encountered such difficulty in defining what, if anything, constitutes the decline they are trying to describe. Its nature and causes have remained contentious for twenty-five years and will doubtless continue to defy precise definition for the foreseeable future. The popularity of Paul Kennedy's book *The Rise and Fall of the Great Powers*, together with the sustained hostility with which its publication was greeted, illustrated how difficult it is to phrase the problem of America's decline in a manner conducive to rational discussion.[7]

Obsessed with the need to escape relegation to the sidelines of history, from which no country has ever regained centre-stage, different interest groups have defined the problem in different ways, each offering the patient dubious nostrums which may yet prove more fatal to recovery than the disease itself.

Politicians appealing to their own constituencies have been eager to communicate their particular concerns to the widest possible public. The Democrats may have been remarkably short of political ideas during the 1988 Presidential campaign but they were quick enough to attack their opponents for overseeing the largest budget and trade deficits in the country's history. For their part, Republicans like Richard Nixon still preferred to trade in causes greater than the nation itself, in the invincible belief that only when a society becomes obsessed with its own material well being to the exclusion of everything else is it 'destined for decline'.[8]

Academics wishing to strike a chord with the 'attentive public', to articulate a popular fear, or even a populist vision have also been forced to cut their cloth to the prevailing political fashion. Theirs is a narrowly based trade. If their works are to escape relegation to the shelves of university libraries, if instead they are to be discussed and debated by the informed public to whom they would like to appeal, their theories have to be universal in application. Their role inevitably has its critics.

'We appear to be living in yet another age', writes Robert Nisbet, 'in which "failure of nerve" is conspicuous not in the minds of America's majority, but in the minds of those who are gatekeepers for ideas and intellectuals'.[9]

Years earlier, Spiro Agnew, Nixon's colourful first Vice President, had also lambasted the 'nattering nabobs of negativism',[10] in keeping with the Administration's belief that everything in Vietnam would be all right but for the manifest *traison des clercs*.

Certainly, Professor Kennedy's book had an impact beyond the significance of the thirty or so pages which he devoted to a discussion of the decline of the United States. An earlier article in *The Atlantic Monthly* had passed almost unnoticed the year before, evidence perhaps that thirty pages of footnotes helped add authority to a view which might otherwise have been dismissed as a journalistic *jeu d'esprit* on the part of a younger member of the profession, or a valedictory reprise in the case of a commentator of the political scene as respected as Henry Brandon.

Intellectual 'fashion' must run deep indeed when there is little real evidence that the United States is in decline, or the evidence is at best conflicting, or even self-fulfilling. It is, in fact, the popular mood—the attractions of decline for a nation weighed down by its international responsibilities which has tended to preclude dispassionate analysis of the question.

Decline is a potent theme for a popular audience. Neo-conservatives find in it a warning for the nation against falling educational standards, the drug culture of the inner cities, the 'decadence' of 'permissive' liberalism. Liberal Democrats, dubious of the Reagan 'renewal', have attacked the foundations of America's economic resurgence while exaggerating the extent to which any administration could arrest, let alone reverse, a country's decline. The story of American politics, after all, is of grand designs ineptly executed, of aspirations on the part of enthusiasts like President Carter who failed to understand or master the political system in time.

Erich Heller has given expression to a mood which is widespread among the intelligentsia, that

the history of the West since 1917 looks like the work of children clumsily filling in with lurid colours a design drawn by Oswald Spengler.

To some extent we are all Spenglerians, doomed to think in the same categories, perhaps even to use the same mental language, to believe no longer in progress but the ineluctable moral decline of Western civilisation.

Governments, notoriously reluctant to respond to public demands, are anxious enough to lead public opinion, aware of the danger that the difference between leading a crowd and being pursued by it can be disconcertingly slight. There may be few, if any, examples of governments voluntarily denying themselves power, but history can furnish occasions on which the public itself has preferred to forfeit political influence, or refused to pick up the bill in order to spare itself the obligations which power brings. In 1964, the United States Congress responded to an attack on a warship in the Gulf of Tonkin, an incident in which not a single life was lost, not even the ship, by authorising President Johnson to begin the bombing of North Vietnam. In 1937, it had chosen to respond to an attack on the gunship *Pannay* in the Yangtse river, an incident in which the ship was sunk with the loss of several lives, by insisting that the Roosevelt Administration withdraw all American warships from Chinese waters.

The perversity of Congress' shifting moods is of account only to the extent that it reflects public opinion. In an age when 9 in 10 Americans are willing to renounce the status of a superpower, in the hope of sharing the burdens of power with allies against whose success they have begun to measure their own nation's decline, the popular perception of decline may be the most important of all.[11] As a concept, whether 'real' or not, it may indeed have something not altogether superficial to say to an age trying to make a style out of despair.

What however, do American politicians, academics or the public at large mean by decline? Do they mean the decline of the *Pax Americana* or the United States itself, or are they referring instead to the passing of an era—the American century which—to quote de Madariaga—has coincided with 'the birth of the world',[12] a world which emerged from the carnage of the First World War from which the United States itself emerged the world's foremost power?

A Nation at Risk

The feeling of national decline obviously runs deep. As President Carter reminded the American people in 1979, the most immediate threat to America's power was a crisis of confidence in the Government, in public institutions, but above all in themselves. It was a problem which de Tocqueville had foreseen in the nineteenth century when he forecast that in their anxiety to make their own fortunes, the Americans might lose sight of the private fortune of each other and the prosperity of all. The idea of self-interest at the heart of the American character, de Tocqueville wrote, was a curious one:

> the better to look after what they call their business they neglect their chief business which is to remain their own masters.[13]

Reagan's promise of renewal seems to bear this prediction out, as young capitalists continue to strip the assets of companies listed on Wall Street, as the country allows foreign interests to buy huge chunks of the American economy, as the Administration persists in financing its defence spending by allowing the Japanese to control a third of the national debt.

Apart from the economic crisis, many Americans have seized upon a number of cultural factors to amplify what they see as the progressive 'closing of the American mind'. In a book which remained on the best seller list for months, Allan Bloom decried the fact that, in their desire to free the United States from prejudice, American liberal educationalists had allowed the country to lapse into a mire of cultural and moral relativism. America, he believed, had reached a stage where 'indiscrimination is a moral imperative because it is the opposite of discrimination'. For a modern nation founded upon the principle of reason 'a crisis in the university, the home of reason, is perhaps the profoundest crisis they face.'[14]

Bloom's voice is not an isolated one. E D Hirsch's *Cultural Illiteracy*, which proved to be another best seller, confirmed a prevailing mood of cultural *angst*. In 1983, four years before Bloom put pen to paper, the Reagan Administration issued a report with the dramatic title of *A Nation at Risk* which diagnosed a 'rising tide of mediocrity' in American schools. Already 10 per cent of Americans are illiterate, the highest percentage in the industrial world. The National Geographical Society commissioned a survey in August 1988 which found that half of America's college students couldn't find Vietnam on a map. Perhaps most disturbing of all is the knowledge of mathematics, in which the United States, for once, trails even behind the Soviet Union. Today, students still read Silvester Thompson's *Calculus made Easy* as part of a two semester college course. When Thompson wrote the book in 1919 it was intended for 16-year-old adolescents.

Citing more examples would be valueless. The problem of ignorance after all is hardly new. Even at the height of the Vietnam War only 25 per cent of Americans were aware that mainland China was under communist rule.[15] During a visit to the United States before the First World War, Rupert Brooke discovered that the students at Harvard were labouring under the impression that Matthew Arnold was still alive: 'I couldn't bring myself to tell [them] that even in Rugby we had forgiven that brilliant youth his iconoclastic tendencies some time ago and that, as a matter of fact, he had died when I was eight months old.'[16]

The critical difference between the past and the present, however, is marked. Something more profound than declining educational standards appears to be at work. Just as the printing press transformed language and behaviour (especially political consciousness) three hundred years ago, so the electronic information revolution seems to have produced a nation whose attention span is strictly limited. American youth appears to have little patience for formal education, and, therefore, fails to read or reason productively. Once they have left school 60 per cent of all American high school children never read another book.

Imperial Retreat?

We can also find structural signs of decline in the *Pax Americana*. The American Empire, in a sense, created the seeds of its own decline by reviving the economies of Western Europe and Japan, while stimulating its own dependence on foreign trade and fixed investment. American scholars on the left have been pre-occupied for so long with Latin America's dependency that they have ignored the signs of America's own dependence on an external economy it once dominated. Between 1946–9 the country's national income doubled; by the late 1950s Germany and Japan were both growing faster than the United States. At the same time, the United States mortgaged its future by running up vast defence budgets, initially to encourage its allies to re-arm.

There is nothing especially 'new', therefore, about America's economic problems. When, in the late 1960s, a rumour that peace was at hand in Vietnam led to a rally on the stock market, it was clear that even those who were committed to the war believed the United States needed to curtail its international commitments to deal with such pressing domestic problems as the deprivation of the inner cities.[17]

Government policies seem merely to have compounded the problem. Carter's Presidency was important for a dramatic shift from unilateral reflation to agreement at the Bonn economic summit (July 1978) to ease up on domestic expansionary policies, which were held responsible for high inflation. Reagan's tax cuts and regulatory reforms produced a massive budget deficit and a burgeoning trade imbalance with the rest of the world which provoked the October 1987 stock market crash. The budget deficit was financed by high interest rates which made the United States an attractive market for foreign investment. In just two years (1983–5), America's capital position switched from that of a leading creditor to leading debtor nation. In relation to its export earnings, the United States is going into debt faster than any major developed country since 1945, and faster than the average of the seven major developing country debtors on the eve of the debt crisis.[18] As *The Washington Post* observed some years ago, America was fortunate that there are no debtor's prisons for nations, for the Reagan Administration's policies had, in a very real sense, forced the country to mortgage its future.[19]

In addition to the immediate effects on the United States economy, the Bretton Woods system, which the United States had put in place in 1944, no longer seems to serve American interests. By the time the Japanese and

Germans emerged as economic powers in their own right, America had become dependent on the system itself. During the 1970s its import and export dependency doubled. Exports rose from 5.7 per cent of GNP (1960) to 12.9 per cent (1980), imports from 4.6 per cent to 12.1 per cent. In 1970, foreign loans amounted to 7.6 per cent of all bank lending; by 1980 they had risen to 26 per cent. US companies had to become more competitive simply to survive. By 1980, one job in six in manufacturing industry depended on overseas markets; one in every three acres of farmland produced crops for export; one dollar in every three of corporate profit derived from exports or foreign investment.[20]

Despite the forecasts of economic Cassandras, however, the fascination with statistics is in itself highly suspicious. The pre-occupation with foreign reserves, trade balances and deficits reflects a more profound loss of confidence in economics itself. One set of figures can always be offset by another. Historically the United States' share of world manufacturing output in the year of the Munich agreement (1938) was lower than at any time since 1910. America's share was lower in 1938 than it had been on the eve of the Great Depression (1929). On this basis, it could have been argued at the time that the United States would eventually be displaced by the Soviet Union whose share of manufacturing output trebled between 1929–38. It could even be argued that its displacement as the dominant economic power was not only inevitable, but not very distant.[21]

In 1981, the United States still accounted for one fifth of global production, and 50 per cent of the world's exports (in dollar terms). As the world's major reserve currency, the dollar was still the medium of exchange for 80 per cent of all non-communist trade and still represented 75 per cent of central bank reserves.[22] The United States is still able to borrow on its own currency. This means that foreigners carry the exchange risk when lending to Washington. At the same time, they are exposed to an exchange risk on their uncovered portfolio of dollar denominated debt issued by other countries, which was estimated to be $800 billion in 1984.[23] We should never forget that, as the world's principal reserve currency, the dollar still provides America with what de Gaulle once called 'the exorbitant privilege' of being able to finance its balance of payments deficits with what are in effect IOUs rather than its own reserve assets.

Even after the 1987 crash, the merchants of doom, in losing confidence in the US economy, tended to lose their heads. Kenneth Galbraith, whose progress to economic depression had been reflected in the titles of his two most important books, *The Affluent Society* and *The Years of Uncertainty*, predicted another Great Depression. Why? Because after the stock market had soared to a historic height of 250 per cent, it dropped by 22 per cent in the course of a day. What Galbraith ignored was the underlying strength of an economy that had produced 16 million more jobs in 64 consecutive months (1982–8); boosted manufacturing productivity to 4.5 per cent a year, the highest rate since 1945, and increased manufacturing output by a factor of four since the late 1970s.

Galbraith, of course, was not alone. At the height of the recession, Albert Bressand wrote of the Williamsburg economic summit (1983) that an Administration that was neither all powerful nor internationally minded could hardly expect to command the type of legitimacy which the *Pax Americana* had originaly conferred.[24] Yet America's recovery from the recession illustrated the extent of the world's dependence on the American economy, in particular American interest rates. In the words of the former President of the Bundesbank, the world saw a 'return to the *Pax Americana*'.[25]

True, America's economic weakness was relative to that of its allies, not its enemies. If, between 1969–79, the Soviet Union devoted almost as great a share of its national product to investment as did Japan, its economy grew at less than half the rate. In the late 1970s, Soviet growth was stagnant. By comparison, the American share of Gross World Product (GWP) may have declined since 1945, yet it still remains larger than that of the Soviet Union and Japan combined, and only marginally smaller than that of the European Community. Far from falling behind Japan in every sphere of economic activity, the United States has managed to hold its own. Since 1982, United States industrial production has been 5 per cent higher than Japan's; its competitiveness in manufacturing has been higher still, which is one reason why the Japanese now manufacture so many of their own cars in America. Labour costs are much lower. United States productivity which was lower even than that of Britain throughout the 1960s and 1970s stands at 29 per cent higher than in 1981, the most prolonged rise in America's history. Ninety per cent of all new jobs created in the Western world since the world came out of the recession, have been created in the United States.

The United States, in fact, is not even a creditor nation if foreign assets are valued correctly. The 'net debt' position reported by the Department of Commerce is based on valuing all investments at book, not market values, a measurement which substantially undervalues the majority of US assets which are more than thirty years old. Assuming a 5 per cent rate of return on investment, the current market value of American holdings abroad exceeds that of foreigners in the United States by $400 billion.[26] In 1986, when the United States supposedly became the largest debtor nation in the world, its income from overseas investment ($20.8 billion) was greater than American payments to foreign creditors and investors. Income earned by Americans on their foreign investments may no longer exceed the income derived by foreigners from their total holdings in the United States, but foreign direct investment (FDI) is still growing faster than world trade (by a margin of 25 per cent or more).

Trade flows, it is true, may still be larger than FDI but such a comparison is a deceptive indicator of a nation's economic performance. A large share of trade is FDI related, representing goods shifted between parent companies and their foreign subsidiaries. For six out of America's ten largest trading partners, the local sales of US-owned companies were larger than American exports to the countries in question.[27]

What of the much discussed budget and trade deficits? These too have been grossly exaggerated. The decision by American bankers to reduce their foreign lendings from $110 billion a year to less than $2 billion in 1985, turned a net creditor into a net debtor nation overnight, providing a sudden stimulus for a trade deficit which was not quite as serious as it appears.[28] As for the budget deficit, which is considered more serious still, that could be eliminated by a marginal increase in direct or indirect taxes. The United States runs it, not because its governments are profligate, not because they are irresponsibly funding public expenditure on welfare entitlements and defence through public borrowing but because the deficit is not that expensive to run.[29]

It is not, of course, economic decline alone which preoccupies Americans.

'The history of the rise and fall of the leading countries in the Great Power system since the advance of Western Europe in the sixteenth century', writes Professor Kennedy, 'shows a very significant correlation over the longer term between productive and revenue raising capacities on the one hand and military strength on the other.'[30]

American expenditure certainly has been marked by a colossal expenditure on arms, accompanied by a rising tide of consumption, fuelled most recently by substantial tax cuts:

It is as though the intercontinental missile and the colour television set reside in the same area of economic expansion. In the modern age you can't keep the two kinds of ingenuity apart—the lethal and the allegedly life enhancing. Indeed, it's possible to sum up part of the age in terms of synthesis of the two ... the cosy television evening with the Vietnam war as part of the chromatic entertainment.[31]

What we are dealing with in the US military is not an industrial complex, but a political community, the Army in particular, which links the United States and Europe in an Atlantic community, that enables the political leadership in the United States to manage the transatlantic bargain in the face of growing opposition from Congress and even public opinion. The Seventh Army provides a cultural underpinning of the American commitment to Europe's defence. It is the Army which permits the transmission of ideas favourable to Atlanticism, a community which is not only congenial to both sides, the European élite as well as the American, but which has bred an unwillingness to share power on the part of one, and an unwillingness to seek a greater degree of independence on the part of the other. The collapse of NATO would be a double catastrophe, for it would not only spell military disaster for the Europeans, but cultural disintegration for those Americans who still wish to transcend narrow political horizons, and isolationist values.

Moreover, is the United States overstretched as Kennedy maintains? 'Imperial overreach' is the most quoted phrase from Kennedy's book, one whose popularity is easily explained 'given that it combines neatly the idea that the United States has an "empire" and that military spending should be cut.'[32] Yet the argument is only acceptable if one believes that the United States lives in a security environment conducive to its survival and well being, one in which the Soviet Union has ceased to pose a threat, in part, because it is in a state of terminal decline. Unfortunately, declining powers tend to be more dangerous than aspiring ones. A country confident it could 'bury' the United States economically by 1980 felt equally confident to cut its armed strength by a million men. A country overtaken in terms of total GNP by Japan in 1986 (possibly much earlier) has increased its arms in all five major armaments categories from tanks to artillery by more than the combined inventories of the Federal Republic of Germany and France (1986–8).

Unlike Great Britain in the 1930s, it may well be the case that the United States finds itself at the head of a coalition of powers, among the wealthiest in the world. The problem is not that the United States spends too much on defence but that it spends too little, given that 55 per cent of GDP is accounted for by welfare entitlements and food stamps, not to mention the 15 per cent or more which is needed every year to service the country's debt. The real problem is that the United States has not derived a proper return on its expenditure because it has spent money with no particular strategic end in mind, in the belief that throwing money at a problem will somehow solve the problem itself. Now that it has engaged on four years of bloodletting to reduce defence spending as a percentage of GNP still further, two questions arise; over its response to burden sharing with its allies, and more important perhaps, its view of its own role in the 1990s.

The United States remains deeply schizophrenic about the first question. On the one hand, it wishes to share its burdens

> 'We hear it said', declared Reagan in his inaugural address, 'that we live in an era of limits to our powers. Well then let it also be understood there are limits to our patience.'

On the other hand, the United States is unlikely to look with relish on a destiny it has to share with others—as Pericles reminded the people of Athens during the Peloponnesian War 'you cannot decline the burdens of empire and still expect to share its honours'.[33] Even in the 1960s, Americans were unwilling to confront this reality. William Fulbright might complain of 'the arrogance of power', but his commitment to the defence of Europe was firmly linked to the need to ensure that 'the critical decisions that lead to war and peace are not removed beyond our influence and responsibility'.[34] 'To conceive destiny as exterior to ourselves . . . a vast cycle of failures is requisite', argued E M Cioran.[35] That may be an unavoidable for a small European power such as Cioran's Romania, but what of a power that has never relied on anyone else for its survival, or fulfilment of its designs?

When Jefferson attributed to Washington the plea for the United States to avoid 'entangling alliances' for fear that the republic would be drawn into conflicts not of its own making, he did not foresee a time when allies might instead prevent the republic from acting on behalf of its own interests. Through its close association with the United States, Europe feels it necessary to caution it against adventurism or the use of force; through association, allied public opinion occasionally feels it necessary to engage in emotional spasms, to demonstrate against American actions such as the bombing of Tripoli (1986) or the invasion of Grenada (1983), by comparison with which the invasion of Afghanistan (1979) drew hardly any protest on the part of European opinion at all.

An adversary's actions invite far less comment. The need to reassure friends is a far more onerous task than deterring enemies. As Ibsen warned 'the trouble with friends is not what they can do for you, but what they prevent you from doing for yourself.' As early as 1980, Henry Kissinger was already complaining that America's military spending no longer bought friends, or kept them on board, and certainly no longer promoted a world in which the United States could feel confident about its own future.[36]

Had Christian Herter's Atlantic Community been realised, the United States might have lived with this dilemma, and even transcended it. Unfortunately, we may expect further anxiety in the United States as the burden-sharing debate gathers momentum. We can interpret it in different ways: we may see it as a failure on the part of the United States to adjust to changing circumstances; or we may see it as the failure of an alliance created by the United States and Britain to adjust to new political realities. What we do know is that the United States is in danger of losing its autonomy in domestic economic problems, now that it relies on a capital inflow of $150 billion to pay its foreign bills, and service its debt. Such a reversal in roles from the days of Marshall Aid suggests that it may not be too long before the Allies preach to their main protector, not the other way round. If the United States should forfeit its authority in the Alliance, if its leadership is questioned, will it lose its 'vocation' as well?

In its rite of passage from a superpower to a great power, America will have to transform its relations with its allies and enemies alike. In NATO it will not only have to revise the transatlantic bargain, by shedding the burdens of empire when it can, it may also have to share power with its European and Japanese allies, to allow them to voice their own opinions, and express their own misgivings more forcefully than they have in the past. It was Walter Lippmann who once suggested that the value of alliances was that, like manacles, they stopped one's hands from shaking. If the Alliance is seen as a fetter, restraining America's energies, the analogy is unlikely to appeal even to a generation which has been encouraged to subscribe to an inverted Catholic litany that preaches that hope is the greatest sin of all. As Irving Kristol has argued quite persuasively, while power may indeed corrupt in the world that exists, rather than the world we might prefer, powerlessness may be far more corrupting and demoralising.[37]

As its power relative to that of its allies begins to ebb, the United States will undoubtedly try to find an option, hopefully a *via media* between 'manic interventionism and depressive withdrawal'.[38] The possibility of withdrawal, however, cannot be discounted. Years before Professor Kennedy put pen to paper, William Fulbright argued that the United States was at a turning point in its history, a point at which great powers tend to lose their perspective on exactly what was within the realm of power and what lay beyond it, a point at which other powers by 'an over-extension of effort' had declined and then fallen.[39] Writing in 1950, Gabriel Almond observed that any underlying doubt in its own strength that was allowed to surface, might leave America with the feeling of being over-extended, a belief that might bring to the fore 'a need for contraction, for consolidation, for withdrawal'.[40]

The most recent opinion polls do not show any return to isolationism, but they do reveal that compared with twenty-five years ago, when a majority of Americans wished the United States to remain at the top, to be 'the very best and looked-up-to nation in the world',[41] a remarkable number now wish it to remain 'uncommitted'.[42]

If the American people were ever to become convinced that their 'decline' was real, they might elect politicians who could best articulate their fears rather than their aspirations. Release from the past might be disastrous in this respect, if no other. It was Alexis de Tocqueville who forecast that the United States would end not with the collapse of its democratic government but the expiry of its energy. Ultimately, he feared not for its want of boldness, but 'the mediocrity of its desires'. Ambition would lose its vigour, passions would abate, society would become less 'aspiring'. So far this has not been the case. Indeed many Americans would sympathise still with the conclusions reached by a group of social scientists in 1957 whose work did much to create the groundwork for the creation of the Development Loan Fund

> if we continue to devote our attention in the same proportion to domestic issues as in the past we run the danger of becoming a bore to ourselves and the world.[43]

America Agonistes, or the passing of the
American Century

Emancipation from the past through recognition of the limits of its power may enable America to come to terms with itself and with the world outside it. Emancipation through decline might also, however, lock the United States into its past more forcefully than ever. As Cioran observed, a country in decline often exits history; if it permits itself a future it frequently does not believe in it. Its sole genius is the genius of nostalgia, a morbid contemplation on the past which is respected more for its own sake, than as a key to unlocking the future.[44]

Is the United States mature enough to adjust to decline, or will it retreat into itself still further? Daniel Bell, who somewhat prematurely forecast the death of ideology in the 1960s, wrote in 1976 that, having aged, the United States now could choose for the first time since the birth of the nation:

> There is no longer a Manifest Destiny or mission. We have not been immune to the corruption of power. We have not been the exception. To a surprising extent there is now a greater range of choice available to the American polity. Our mortality now lies before us.[45]

The problem is what choice will America make? It can look back or it can look forward. It can become an 'ordinary' country or remain wedded to a historical ideal. It can see in the past 'a body of beliefs the prison from which escape is hazardous' (to quote the most distinguished historian of manifest destiny),[46] or it can attempt to enter history for the first time by rising above its mythical past.

The United States has always seen itself as a country outside history, a hero, always solitary, its ambitions always excessive. In the end the hero traditionally returns, his mission completed or unrealised. 'The man whose life is an ordeal of self-examination', writes Paul Zweig of the heroic ideal in literature, 'needs in the end to be included once again'.[47] Being a hero is a solitary and forlorn business. As one of Pasternak's characters says in *Dr Zhivago* about the communist leadership, they aren't 'happy with anything unless it is on a world scale. For them the transitional periods, worlds in the making, are an end in themselves . . .' a position he finds ludicrous because man is born to live, not to prepare for life.

Does the United States wish to remain heroic? Possibly not. Decline, as the Mexican writer, Octavio Paz argues, is the Americans' gateway to history; for it 'offers them what they have always sought; historical legitimacy.'[48] Having discovered mortality, the United States can now 'unblushingly identify itself with the great empires of the past.'

> The United States would like to be outside the world, but it is in the world—it *is* the world. Hence the contradiction of contemporary American society;

being at once an empire and a democracy is the result of another, deeper contradiction, having been founded against history, yet being itself history.[49]

Just as the Soviet Union has been forced to come to terms with its own inability to play the role of a historical agent, giving history a push as a superpower, as Suslov used to put it, so the United States has begun to question the role conferred on it by the Founding Fathers; that of an actor outside history, an example to some, a crusader to others, a country which would ultimately redeem Twain's 'damned human race'. America in that respect has always been condemned to play the role of Pytor Chaadaev's Russia in 1829:

> We are one of those nations which do not appear to be an integral part of the human race, but exist only in order to teach some great lesson to the world. Surely the lesson we are destined to teach will not be wasted; but who knows when we shall rejoin the rest of mankind and how much misery we must suffer before accomplishing our destiny.[50]

For two centuries the United States saw itself as a country once removed from the historical constraints within which others had to manoeuvre for advantage, or survive by cunning. It constantly was spurred on by the dynamic urge to occupy 'empty spaces . . . and that space more empty still, the future'.[51] There was even a moment when some Americans believed the Fall could have been averted if Adam had had the good sense to consume the serpent rather than the apple.[52] By the end of his life Twain's misanthropy had got the better of him. De Tocqueville had once written that North America had been discovered 'as if it had been kept in reserve by the Deity and had just risen from beneath the waters of the Deluge'.[53] With the Biblical analogy very much in mind, Twain admitted that were he ever to be appointed Recording Angel, he would have no hesitation in unleashing a second Flood, ensuring that this time there would be no remission; no Noah, no Ark.[54]

Decline offers the United States an entry back into history, an opportunity to escape its messianic role, and become 'an ordinary country' like any other.[55] Not everyone relishes the prospect, of course. Reading the memoirs of men like George Ball, or George Kennan, the theme that emerges most clearly is one of opportunities that were lost, a glimpse of a world that might have been, the aspirations of an élite that felt duty-bound to make the world safe for democracy, or to push the developing world into self-sustained economic growth. The importance of such views arises not from the number of policymakers who shared them, but the fact that they were a significant segment of an educated, talented, sensitive and conscientious group—men who gave leadership and direction to the causes they espoused so notably. Frustration, not isolation, was the experience of such men, frustration of having employed their talents to the full when in office only to see their achievement fall far short of their own hopes. Their present fear is that if the United States turns its back on its past, it will pass into history with its great tasks left unfinished, its debts unpaid, its accounts in disorder, and its image as a redeeming nation, not a little patined, if not faintly tarnished.

For those seeking release from the past, the picture is very different. For them the period when the United States was most in command of its future was before 1917, when it first aspired to become a great power. Whether one reads the speeches of Senator Taft on the right of the political spectrum, or the polemics of Noam Chomsky on the left, it is clear that America's decline followed almost immediately upon its decision to leave Eden, to venture into the corrupting world of great power politics whose rules were foreign to its nature.

For all their criticism of wars such as Vietnam, their message is not one of commitments too many, but of commitments which should never have been undertaken. Hoover opposed America's membership of NATO because it would distort the country's economic development, Taft because of his belief that crusades had no place in the modern world; that protected by high tariff walls and fortified by neutrality, the struggle against communism could be pursued with equal vigour at home.

The emergence of the country as a superpower heralded a false dawn, not a new identity. The end of America's innocence was its true decline. George Urban detected in Kennan's 1957 Reith Lectures, in which he had called on the United States to divest itself of nuclear weapons, to rely for its safety on 'God's grace and our good conscience', a puritanical sense of guilt, a feeling that the United States had become too rich and too powerful, guilt above all because it had not suffered what other nations had suffered from the beginning of time.[56] True to the traditions of the Founding Fathers, Kennan had seen the United States in 1947 as Cellorigo had seen Castille on the eve of Spain's rise as a great power 'a republic of bewitched beings living outside the natural order of things,'[57] a state of affairs which could not last for ever.

If the American century is coming to an end, there are those who would argue its end is not terminal, but transitory, an *entr'acte* to a 'new beginning', one concerned with consequences as well as initiatives.[58] For those for whom the United States has not yet escaped its adolescence, decline offers a key to the wisdom of old age. In *The Power and the Glory* Greene once wrote 'there is always one moment in childhood when the door opens and lets the future in . . .' the future with all its betrayals, petty compromises and glimpses of lost innocence.

The United States may also have to become less introverted, less insensitive to changes going on around it even in the Western Hemisphere. It has always been an intensely solipsistic country, in which its own values have formed the one fixed reference point in its moral universe. Shorn of its past, if it is not to be denied a future it will have to change its ways. Unfortunately, the last election campaign suggested that it is unlikely to throw up a political leader capable of articulating a new vision. In Bush and Dukakis it discovered two putative Presidents whose grammar was peculiarly American, who spoke in a tense the English language does not allow: 'the imaginary present.'

Bush's faith in SDI as 'an exit from mankind's dilemma in which security and survival remained linked' was a classic form of escapism.[59] Dukakis's belief in the United States as the exemplar of the age betrayed a singular unwillingness to accept that there was anything 'ordinary' about the republic at all.

The two outsiders in the primary campaign, Pat Robertson and Jesse Jackson, one a conservative religious fundamentalist, the other a fiery advocate of the black community, preached a message even more irrelevant to America's place in time, a message which was essentially ahistorical. Neither the promise of Jackson's Rainbow Coalition nor the aspirations of the Moral Majority offered a way into history, only a way out. Jackson's defence agenda: 'we have guided missiles but unguided minds', whilst a repudiation of American policy since the 1950s, offered no future prescriptions at all. His thesis that the multinational banks and corporations had forged a new global order that had replaced unionised labour at home with slave labour abroad, his vision of the United States as a country victimised by 'merger maniacs', 'corporate barracuda' and 'chemical warfare' (i.e. pollution and industrial waste) put him far to the left of McGovern, Henry Wallace and even Eugene Debs.[60]

What the United States needs most is not a deeply visionary leader, a prophet without honour in a country recognisable only to his supporters, but a pragmatist willing to trek towards an unknown future, a task the American people might find more beguiling than Reagan's historical rally. In a word—the Americans need a politician of the 1990s, not the leader of an ebbing superpower masquerading in yesterday's clothes.

If decline holds out hope for radical Americans who would like to return to the innocence of the past, and equal hope for a generation that would like to be spared its obligations, it also offers the informed public a re-interpretation of America's past which might one day lead to its repudiation. In re-writing the past, however, will the American people contract into history at the expense of their friends? The danger of becoming an ordinary country is that the transformation may generate fears that are more acute than real, that are magnified, not muted, a sense of collective despair which may make political abdication preferable to political responsibility.

As Cioran once wrote, a minimum of unconsciousness is necessary if one wishes to stay inside history. To act is one thing; to know one is acting, quite another. A man lives by fictions; the man who unmasks them renounces his own identity and in a sense himself. Any other fictions he may later accept, in originating outside his own experience, may deny his own personality.

> How much more so this applies to a civilisation which vacillates as soon as it exposes the errors which permitted its growth and its lustre as soon as it calls into question its own truths ... when the sceptic no longer extracts any active virtue from his problems and interrogations, he approaches his *dénouement*, indeed seeks it out. ...[61]

Faced with this bleak prospect, perhaps, the United States would be well advised in the case of scholars such as Professor Kennedy to ban their books, or even burn them, or better still, to follow the sound advice of Heine—who wanted to imprison every prophet of doom until such time as their prophecies came true.

Notes

1. Joseph A Schumpeter *Capitalism, Socialism and Democracy*. New York: Harper and Row, 1942, pp. 131–9. For Toynbee see *Hannibal's Legacy Volume 2: Rome and her neighbours after Hannibal's exit*. Oxford University Press, 1965 'In fact the after effects of the Hannibalic bout of the Romano-Carthaginian Double War were not solely military; they were economic, social and religious as well. This was the price of Rome's subjugation of the western end of the old world-oikoumene. It was a price that condemned the Roman Empire in advance to be short lived', p. 9.
2. Andrew Hacker *The End of the American Era*. New York: Atheneum, 1970, p. 230.
3. Ronald Steel *Pax Americana*. New York: Viking, 1967, p. 45.
4. Donald Brandon *American foreign policy: beyond utopianism and realism*. New York, Appleton and Century Croft, 1966, pp. 269–89.
5. Henry Brandon *The Retreat of American Power*. New York: Doubleday, 1973, p. 360.
6. *Ibid.* p. 346.
7. Paul Kennedy *The Rise and Fall of the Great Powers: economic change and military conflict from 1500 to 2000*. New York: Random House, 1987.
8. *The Sunday Times*, 2 October 1988.
9. Robert Nisbet *History of the Idea of Progress*. New York: Basic Books, 1980, p. 197.
10. Cited William O'Neil *Coming Apart: an informal history of America in the 1960's*. New York: Quadrangle, 1971, p. 405.
11. Mellman and Lazarus *Research defining American strength: results of a Survey conducted for the World Policy Institute*. October 1987, p. 14.
12. Salvador de Madariaga *Americans*. Oxford University Press, 1930, p. 3.
13. Alexis de Tocqueville *Democracy in America*. (tr) Phillips Bradley: New York: Knopf, 1945, Volume 2, p. 141.
14. Allan Bloom *The Closing of the American Mind*. New York: Simon and Schuster, 1987.
15. Lloyd Free/Hadley Cantril *The political beliefs of Americans: a study of Public Opinion*. New York: Simon and Schuster, 1968, p. 50.
16. Rupert Brooke *Letters from America*. Gloucester: Alan Sutton, 1984, p. 46.
17. Richard D Challenger 'The next President's foreign policy legacy'. University—*Princeton Quarterly No. 69*. Summer 1976, pp. 11–12.
18. Stephan Marris *Deficits and Dollars: the world economy at risk*. Washington DC: Institute for International Economics, 1985, p. 94.
19. *The Washington Post*, 7 October 1985.
20. Fred Bergsten 'The cost of Reaganomics', *Foreign Policy No. 44*, Fall 1981, p. 36.
21. Owen Harries 'The rise of American decline', *Commentary* 85:5, May 1988, p. 32.
22. Robert Ayres 'Breaking the Bank' *Foreign Policy No. 43*, Summer 1981, pp. 104–20.

23. Marris *Deficits and dollars, op. cit.* p. 371.
24. Albert Bressand 'Mastering the world economy', *Foreign Affairs* 61:4, Spring, 1982, pp. 761–2.
25. Cited Sam Brittan 'A very painful world adjustment', *Foreign Affairs* 61:3, p. 547.
26. *National Review*, 7 November 1988, p. 14.
27. *The Times*, 17 November 1988.
28. Warren T Brooks 'The silent boom', *The American Spectator*. August 1988, p. 18.
29. It is often suggested that were America to tax itself at a much higher rate, it could ease the budget deficit quite speedily. Over time ideas change. It is possible, however, to ignore Madison and cite Jefferson instead, not the Jefferson who supported the democratic collectivists against the private monopolies—but the Jefferson who went on to insert a note into de Tracy's Treatise on Political Economy (1817) which he recommended as a text book for the University of Virginia. The note read 'The use of taxing power to correct inequalities of wealth violates the first principle of society, the guarantee to everyone of a free exercise of his industry and the fruits acquired by it', Frank Tariello *The reconstruction of American political ideology*. Charlottesville, University of Virginia Press, 1982, p. 13.
30. Kennedy *Rise and Fall of the Great Powers, op. cit.* p. 316.
31. Anthony Burgess *1985*. London: Arrow, 1985, p. 63.
32. Harries *Rise of American Decline, op. cit.* p. 34.
33. William Fulbright *Prospects for the West*. Cambridge, Mass: Harvard University Press, 1963, p. 57.
34. E M Cioran *The Temptation to Exist*. London: Quartet, 1987, p. 70.
35. Nowhere in Washington's Farewell Address is the phrase 'entangling alliances' to be found. It was first introduced in Jefferson's inaugural address of 1801.
36. Henry Kissinger: Address before the annual Convention of American Society of Newspaper Editors, Washington DC, April 10 1980.
37. *The Wall Street Journal*, 18 January 1979.
38. Sewell in Russet *No Clear and Present Danger*, p. 94.
39. William Fulbright *The Arrogance of Power*. New York: Random House, 1966, p. 3.
40. Almond *The American People and Foreign Policy*. New York: Harcourt Bruce, 1950, p. 65.
41. Lloyd Free and Hadley Cantril *The Political Beliefs of Americans*. New York: Simon and Schuster, 1968, p. 92.
42. John Reilly 'American opinion: continuity not Reaganism', *Foreign Policy* 50, (Spring 1982), pp. 86–104.
43. Max Millikan/Walt Rostow *A Proposal's key to an effective foreign policy*. New York: Harper, 1957, p. 150.
44. Cioran *The Temptation to Exist, op. cit.* p. 68.
45. Daniel Bell 'The end of American exceptionalism', Nathan Glazer/Irving Kristol, *The American Commonwealth—1976*. New York: Basic Books, 1976.
46. Alstyne *The American Empire: its historical pattern and evolution*. London: Historical Association, 1960, p. 28.
47. Paul Zweig *The Heresy of Self-Love: a study of subversive individualism*. New Jersey: Princeton University Press, 1960, p. 174.
48. Octavio Paz *One Earth, Four or Five Worlds: reflections on contemporary history*. Carcanet: 1985, pp. 22–3.
49. *Ibid.* p. 31–2.
50. Brzezinski *Power and Principle: the memoirs of the National Security Adviser, 1977–81*. London: Weidenfeld & Nicolson, 1983, p. 541.
51. Paz *One Earth, op. cit.* p. 36.
52. Mark Twain *'Pudden' head Wilson*. New York: Bantam Books, 1984, p. 6.
53. Alexis de Tocqueville *Democracy in America, op. cit.* Volume 1, p. 302.
54. Janet Smith (ed) *Mark Twain on the Damned Human Race*. New York: Hill and Wang, 1962, p. 3.
55. Richard Rosencrance *America as an Ordinary Country*. New York: Cornel University Press, 1976.
56. George Urban (ed) *Encounters with George Kennan: the great debate*. London: Frank Cass, 1979, p. 24.

57. J H Elliott 'The decline of Spain' in C M Cipolla (ed) *The economic decline of empires.* London: Methuen, 1970, p. 195.

58. John Montgomery *Aftermath: tarnished outcomes of American foreign policy.* Auburn House Publishing, 1986, p. 110.

59. George Bush 'Moral aspect of Deterrence' Speech at Fordham University, New York, 28 April 1983 Cited Raymond Shulsted *Peace is my profession: a soldier's view of the moral dimension of US Nuclear Policy.* Washington DC: National Defence University Press, 1986, p. 18.

60. See Paul M Gigot 'The Jackson package' *The American Spectator,* June 1986, pp. 14–16.

61. Cioran *Temptation to Exist, op. cit.* pp. 55–6.

PART 2

American Responsibilities and Global Security: Two Views from the United States

CHAPTER 3

The Bush Administration

LAWRENCE EAGLEBURGER

This chapter addresses itself to some of the more serious foreign policy challenges the Western Alliance will face, not so much in terms of the next six months or the next Administration, but as the United States and its allies try to move in a constructive way into the twenty-first century. In looking at some of the problems that the West is likely to confront, it might be useful to quote from a speech I gave in 1987.

Europeans, or at least those over fifty years of age, know as no American can, that the twentieth century has not been a vintage era in human history. Indeed, the American historian, Barbara Tuchmann, argued with substantial justice that we must go back to the fourteenth century to find a period as unstable and bloody as our own times. Two world wars, the deaths of tens of millions in those wars, a disastrous depression, the rise and fall of national socialism, the end of colonialism with its attendant instability and economic chaos, and the rise of communist totalitarianism all are evidence of the abysmal failure of most of those who led in the West, particularly in Europe, from the close of the nineteenth century through the first four decades of the twentieth century. Our common task—Western Europe's and America's—since the end of the Second World War has been, above all else, to see that the errors that marked that time are not repeated again by this or succeeding generations.

By any reasonable standard, we have done not badly so far. Europe has enjoyed a longer period of peace than at any time in the past 100 years, thanks largely to the NATO Alliance and the commitment of the United States to the defence of its allies. Together we have built a host of institutions, particularly in the economic arena, that have established a commonly accepted set of rules which have mitigated the worst aspects of unilateralism and unfettered nationalism. Bretton Woods, the IMF, the IBRD, the GATT, the OECD and the European Community have all played a major role in leading the industrial democracies toward a far more rational international economic order than history has known before. The Western democracies, then, have much about which to congratulate themselves. And we Americans have a right to be

43

particularly proud of the part played—a role unique not only in our own history, but in world history as well.

We now need to ask whether, as we move farther from the bad old days of 1939–1945, the commitment to common goals and the institutions that have made it possible for us to work together toward these goals, remains as strong as it has been. Regrettably, I am of the view that it does not—on either side of the Atlantic. Over the past decades there has been a slow deterioration of the dedication to what I will call the Transatlantic idea and with it a lessened commitment to multilateral co-operation. We find it ever more difficult to expand the scope of existing international institutions or to build new ones to meet the challenges of an increasingly complex world— challenges that we all know will grow more dangerous as we move toward the twenty-first century.

Nuclear arms control, for example, has mesmerised us for years but how much time have we spent seeking collective solutions to the perhaps equally dangerous and less containable problems of the developing world? Have any of us had the courage to call for a new joint approach to the growing international debt crisis? Are any of us really ready to make the sacrifices necessary to counter the threat of protectionism? Are we ever going to find the common will to overcome the Soviet Union's substantial conventional arms superiority, particularly now that we seem on the way to reducing the size of our nuclear deterrent? I could go on, but the point is clear. The West runs the danger of entering the next century plagued once again by the same failure of will and creativity that marked the transition from the nineteenth to the twentieth centuries. It's against that background that I would like to address some of the challenges which will face us as we move into the twenty-first century, starting briefly with some of the 'traditional' challenges while suggesting that 'traditional' solutions are not necessarily the right ones.

First of all, the relationship with the Soviet Union is changing. We all know what is apparently in the process of change within the Soviet Union itself. In 1987, we saw a President of the United States walking arm in arm with Gorbachev through Red Square, a vision which would have been unthinkable a few years ago. There are few in the West who do not wish Gorbachev well with *perestroika* and *glasnost*, but I would suggest that there are too many in the West who are prepared to jump to conclusions which, as yet, are hard to support on the basis of the evidence available.

There is no question that Gorbachev is sincere in his attempts to reform the Soviet economic system and, perhaps, its political system as well. It is, I think, equally clear that the reason for this is that he has understood, as I think Andropov did before him, that the Soviet economic system is in terrible shape; that the Soviet Union clearly will not be able to compete with the West as it moves into the twenty-first century unless there are some substantial changes. It is equally right, however, to ask ourselves whether it is possible that, in his attempt at reform, Gorbachev will fail and that he will be followed in his failure by someone who will be much more difficult to deal with. I don't know of any Soviet expert within the United States Government or outside it who is convinced that the answer is either that Gorbachev will succeed or that he will fail. Most Soviet experts in the United States are about evenly divided on whether he will remain in power over a protracted period of time. As long as it is not clear that he can succeed, it would seem to me the better part of wisdom to remember that there is no constitutional method of changing power in the Soviet Union and that, as a consequence, if Gorbachev is deposed, there is no guarantee that his successor will carry out any of the objectives or commitments made by the present General Secretary.

A second question we need to ask ourselves is whether it is necessarily in the West's interests to have a more effective adversary. Until we see the beginnings of substantial change in the way in which the Soviet Union conducts its affairs abroad, it would seem wiser to be cautious in our dealings with the Soviet Union. From our point of view, it is Soviet external conduct which is the most important element against which we must judge our own relationship with Moscow. I would warn the Europeans that the vision of Ronald Reagan, the most conservative President of the United States since Herbert Hoover, holding out the vision of a world free of all nuclear weapons, set a standard for a more liberal successor which it will be hard to reverse. With a public which will probably look at the Soviet threat as substantially diminished, substantial defence budgets will not be an easy thing for the present Administration to accomplish. The atmosphere of summitry, the charm of Gorbachev's personality, and the interest on the part of most Western European countries to continue the process of 'detente' lead me to the view that we will see a continuation of a less than well reasoned approach to the Soviet Union.

Whatever the Bush Administration may do, however, it also seems likely that United States' policy toward the Soviet Union over the course of the next fifteen years will more or less remain consistent with the policies of the past. We will be engaged in arms control negotiations, no question about that, but the fundamentals of the relationship, the fundamentals of one defence policy, and the ways in which the West in general, and the United States in particular, try to deal with that relationship are not likely to change significantly in the foreseeable future.

The second traditional challenge that we face relates to the relationship between Western Europe and the United States. While I am not a prophet of doom, I am of the view that there has been a fairly steady increase in transatlantic strains. So far these have affected attitudes more than actions on either side of the Atlantic. Over time, however, unless we do something to reverse the process, they may lead to some changes in the way in which we deal with each other across the Atlantic. The reasons for these increasing strains, I think, are not hard to understand. They are, in part, generational as Europe and the United States move further away from 1945. I would argue as well, that the global nature of the United States' role, as against the more or less regional nature of European interests, has itself let to substantial differences of view on a number of issues which themselves have then led to strain across the Atlantic, notably over the Tripoli raid (1986), for example. My argument is not whether we were right or wrong, but rather that when we act in the context of what we see to be an issue important to our global strategic situation, it often runs against the grain as far as the Europeans are concerned.

Until recently, I would have said that differences in the perception of the Soviet threat were a cause of strain. Before, it was a question of Europe looking at a benighted American Administration that, with its view of the 'evil empire', was thought to be unnecessarily harsh. Now that the United States has put the evil empire aside and has decided that Alice may in fact live in Wonderland, there is substantial nervousness, at least in some quarters in Europe, that we have ignored their interests and have moved too fast to reach agreement with the Soviet Union. The Reykjavik summit in 1986 certainly gave Europeans perfectly legitimate reasons for that concern. It was totally unprofessional and clearly demonstrated that the Reagan Administration, when it found it convenient to do so, was prepared to forget that it had European allies who deserved to be consulted before it made sweeping decisions.

Fortunately for the West, Gorbachev made a major mistake and didn't take up the President's offer. If he had, we would all be in substantial trouble. As it was, Reykjavik certainly had an impact on the way in which Europeans look at America's ability to maintain a steady course.

On the other hand, there is, as well, in the United States a substantial and growing frustration with what Americans perceive to be Europe's unwillingness to accept its responsibilities and carry its fair share of the defence burden. Frequently the Americans are misinformed. Until they recognise that the Federal Republic of Germany, for example, still has a draft and the United States does not, the US is likely to look and to act with regard to its European allies in an unnecessarily confrontational way.

Having said that, I would add that there is justice in the basic American view that Western Europe, with a GNP and population greater than that of the Soviet Union, should, at some reasonable point in the future, be able to carry a greater responsibility for its own defence.

What we see today in terms of movement in Europe towards a single integrated market by the end of 1992 offers hope to those Americans who believe that Europe must involve itself more in the business of building Europe. If the process of building that market leads toward the development of a Western Europe that is able to carry, in a collective sense, a greater burden that is to the good, and in the long run will strengthen the transatlantic relationship. If, however, that single market becomes a protectionist market as far as the United States is concerned, it will open a Pandora's box that we should all prefer remain closed. If that is what is built, then Europe will give the protectionists in America a tremendous argument in their favour. If economic conditions in the United States deteriorate, we could then see a serious attempt at major protectionist measures by the US Congress.

The next semi-traditional problem is Japan. And here there are two kinds of issues. There are the immediate issues of trade and defence where the Americans aided, abetted and encouraged by Europe, spend a great deal of time discussing Japanese trade practices, most of which are, indeed, less than philanthropic. The Japanese have made it clear they do not really understand how to deal with the United States and probably with Western Europe. But that said, what this argument in the United States has led us to is something towards which we too often have a tendency anyway—a failure to look at our own delinquencies, and to ascribe to the Japanese all the basic causes of our trade imbalance. It ought to be fairly clear to most Americans that while they may not be able to expect the 'fair play' from Japan that they constantly demand, unless they are prepared to set their own house in order in ways that they have thus far not been prepared to do, it will really not make much difference whether the Japanese open their markets to the United States or not. The trade imbalance will continue because, too often, the Japanese simply do a better job than the rest of us.

Another issue on which we Americans spend a great deal of time is the question of Japan's insufficient expenditure on defence. It would be unique in history if a country as powerful economically as Japan were forever to eschew military power. To encourage the process, however, is close to insane. If we continue to demand increased expenditure on defence, what we will find before too long is that we have encouraged the Japanese to be as effective in the production of arms and their sale to countries around the world as they have been in making and selling cassette decks, CD players, and computer chips. I do not think it is in the interests of the West to spend any time at all pushing the Japanese toward a greater defence role. What is important, and what the United States and its European allies need to think about, is how we can bring Japan into a more constructive role, in co-operation with the rest of us, in dealing with a whole host of problems which the United States can no longer address alone.

I am talking most of all about assistance to the developing world. But it goes beyond that. It ought not be a question simply of meeting with the Japanese Prime Minister in the Group of Seven to persuade him to put another $20 billion into the aid budget. It ought to be a question of how we can collectively begin to bring an insular people to accept a broader sense of their general responsibilities, so that the Japanese may begin to see themselves in a different light in terms of the role they should play on the world scene.

I am the first to admit that all this is far more easily said than done. There is some evidence, however, that a younger generation of Japanese has begun to think differently from its predecessors; there is some evidence that a younger generation of Japanese have begun to say that the way in which they have organised their internal economy, with heavy emphasis on saving and very light emphasis on consumer goods and consumer benefits, must change. As I am no expert, I have no idea how to further that process, but I would suggest that it is something on which the Western democracies ought collectively to spend more time. If we do not find ways to bring Japan into a more constructive relationship, we run two risks. First, we deny ourselves both the technological skill and imagination of a very creative people, as well as the money that is potentially available to help us bear the burden of assisting the developing world. Second, we run the risk of seeing a Japan by the end of the century or early into the next century that has reduced its relationship with the United States and Western Europe and begun to look more toward the People's Republic of China and a semi-independent role in South-East Asia. Neither would be in our interests.

Let me move briefly now from those more traditional challenges to what I erroneously describe as 'new challenges'. They are not new, it's only that they are getting to the point where they can no longer be ignored. Most of them relate in one way or another to the developing world. I am especially concerned at the degree to which the West, in its concern about its own problems, has failed in any constructive way to begin to think about how to deal with that portion of the world which, if we are not careful, will become more unstable than it already is.

I should add that my concern is far less that within the next ten years the Soviet Union will send its divisions across the dividing line between East and West Europe. Rather, it is that we will, if we do not deal with these potential instabilities, find ourselves inadvertently in confrontation with the Soviet Union in some unexpected backwater, just as two alliance systems did at Sarajevo.

The first of these problems and the one that we all know most about is the debt issue. I regret to say that of all Western governments it was the United States—until the Baker Plan—that was least prepared to consider this problem in a new way. It was the United States that was most prepared to say that the way to deal with this question was to reschedule the debt rather than move toward more radical solutions. I am not sure how much longer a major portion of the developing world can contemplate with equanimity continuing to pay the interest on its debt without even getting at the issue of the principal, when the cost of that expenditure is little or no domestic economic growth.

It is also true that, since a number of these countries are budding democracies, the risk we run is increasing economic instability which leads to a discrediting of the democratic parties and a move to left authoritarianism.

A related issue, and one that deserves a great deal of consideration, is that of technological change—the world of hi-technology we will be living in the twenty-first century. Information technology, particularly, will have a major impact; we have only begun to see the changes that will come from the fact that we will have in our hands, on one disc, a compilation of information that was inconceivable in an earlier age. The very fact of having that information readily available will itself create a new knowledge. It may mean a major change in the way in which we in the West live, not unlike the changes that television has made in our own lifetime. It is clear to me that this concern with technology is a driving factor in what Gorbachev is attempting to do in the Soviet Union. He understands the need to come to grips with the technology revolution particularly as it relates to information technology.

New technology also offers possibilities for the developing world to deal in new ways with some of its economic problems—if we are wise in the ways in which we try to share that technology. If, on the other hand, we do not manage that sharing we will find the gap between the developed and the developing world increasing, which, again, will threaten political stability.

As an American, I am even more concerned that, by the end of the century, the most serious foreign policy problem facing the United States may be Mexico. It is not simply that Mexico is debt-ridden and in serious economic trouble. Far more serious is the fact that its political structure is under increasing pressure. The party that has governed since the Mexican revolution is increasingly out of touch with those constituencies that it has been able to represent so effectively for so long. What we are seeing is a northern tier of Mexican states where businessmen oriented toward the North dominate, with a central area increasingly poverty-stricken, and a south which is at best only entering the twentieth century. This, plus a birth rate which is beyond comprehension, has produced two kinds of pressures.

The first is illegal immigration into the United States which has created its own problems. More fundamental, however, is the question of how much longer we can expect that the Mexican situation can drift, with a régime that is less and less capable of governing, before there are major problems of instability. If this should happen, the Europeans would be well advised to think about the impact on the way in which the United States would look at the rest of the world. If, for the first time since 1847, the US has really serious political instability on its southern border, America may, because its attention will be riveted there, move toward a kind of neo-isolationism that will only serve the interests of one's enemies.

I am drawing a much more pessimistic picture than I believe likely. I am doing so in order to suggest that the 'Third World problem' which we all talk about while rarely knowing what we mean, can be narrowed down to some specific examples. If we are not prepared to deal with the problem collectively, we are in for serious trouble. If we do act together, the issue is containable.

Let me sum up by saying that all of the problems I have described are manageable, not soluble, but manageable if, collectively, we have the wit to deal with them. I use the word 'collectively' because it goes back to my first point in this chapter. What concerns me is that, having learned the lessons of the disasters of the first half of the twentieth century, we now run the risk of repeating them. In the period 1945–1965 we learned that problems can be managed through collective effort and institutions. The challenges I have described are only open to solution by collective measures. Unless we are able to raise our sights and to begin to talk about some of the common problems that may yet defeat us, if we don't recognise that they need to be dealt with in a common way, we are in for a very bad time indeed. As Benjamin Franklin said at the beginning of the American revolution, 'Gentlemen, either we hang together or we will hang separately.'

CHAPTER 4

The Congress of the
United States

JIM MOODY

It's clear that there are tremendous changes which have gradually taken place within NATO. The American public is only dimly aware of these trends but will, from time to time, suddenly recognise that basic realities have shifted. It perceives NATO through snapshots, as though from a movie picture, snapshots which encourage the American public to look at NATO anew.

In recent months these snapshots show Americans that the following changes have taken place. (1) The United States now plays a far less dominant role in the world economy than in past decades; (2) the European nations are far stronger economically than they once were, relative to us; (3) our friends are military and political friends who are, in fact, our trading competitors; (4) the growing economic and political cohesion within Europe has not been matched by growing military cohesion—witness the French and Spanish separations.

Of these snapshot observations, I would say the economic ones are most dominant in United States thinking. Clearly, informed and constructive American policy must be rooted in American public opinion and I will try to sketch briefly five key elements of American attitudes towards NATO as I perceive them at this time.

First, NATO remains an important ally of the United States and the European countries within NATO remain extremely important in a political and military sense to the United States. There has been no disillusionment with NATO. There has been no disaffection. The discussion about the Alliance seems to focus on peripheral issues rather than on its central value—issues such as how much spending Americans should be laying out in the European theatre; what forms of spending; what weapons mix; and whether or not burden sharing is a valid concept. These are the discussions which seem to be taking place. They are not fundamental. NATO remains a centrepiece of American foreign policy in the minds of the public.

Second, there is a feeling that the United States needs to spend less money on defence in Europe while the other countries in Europe need to spend more. Obviously, we have budget pressures in the United States. We have an unbelievable budget deficit. We have a trade deficit with most of our European allies. We have a perception that European economies are relatively strong and that American military budgets over the last few years have been larger than necessary. There is a growing sense that bloated US military budgets could be reduced without an appreciable reduction in security. One might conclude that we need to spend less everywhere but most attention focuses on Europe because it is there that our allies are far stronger than when we last noticed.

A poll conducted in March 1988 showed that Americans, by a two to one margin, believe that our economic competitors world-wide, including Europe, pose a greater threat to American security than our military adversaries.[1] There is a perception in the United States that our real need is economic security. Asked whether economic power was just as important as military power, 59 per cent of Americans strongly agreed with that statement and 29 per cent agreed somewhat, from an overall total of 78 per cent agreeing that economic power is just as important as military power.[2] Almost 9 out of every 10 Americans want to reduce United States defence spending by 'requiring the Japanese, the Koreans and the Europeans to pay for their own defense.'[3] Obviously, the results are altered by the inclusion of Japan and Korea. It isn't a clear-cut question in NATO but does indicate a general perception that our European allies ought to pay more for their own defence.

Let me elaborate a little more on the burden-sharing question. There are three cautionary points worth noting.

First, the burden-sharing debate touches a raw nerve in America—the polls I have just described tend to support the perception that the United States cannot sustain the tremendous level of military spending without genuinely hurting its own economy. That isn't just an opinion; it is an objective fact. The burden-sharing issue will continue to dog the Alliance either until we can successfully redistribute the burden or reduce it by arms control, conventional reductions or other measures.

My second is that American influence will decline as the burden shifts. It will come as a rude awakening to many Americans that reduced spending on NATO means correspondingly reduced influence within NATO. I don't believe this matter has been thought through yet by the American public. Surprisingly, an October 1987 poll found that, by a margin of 51 per cent to 35 per cent, Americans would prefer the United States to be one of several leading nations, co-operating with one another than remaining 'the number one' military and economic leader.[4] Will they find it as appealing in practice?

My third burden-sharing caution involves reassurance. The United States must reassure its NATO allies in Europe that diminished military spending does not lead necessarily to a diminished commitment to European security. There is a belief that we can probably do as well with less (for a variety of reasons which I will touch upon later).

I believe that the United States needs to spend less and European countries more on security. I also believe that the massive military confrontation in Europe must be reduced through arms control. The enormous accumulation of military hardware and manpower by the East and West in an otherwise peaceful part of the world is increasingly perceived as an anachronism, an historic accident, not necessarily reflecting modern realities. The former MBFR negotiator, US Ambassador Jonathan Dean, has called for a 'building down' of the confrontation in Europe. The perception of the Soviet threat and the likelihood of a Soviet invasion has diminished. Yet both NATO and the Warsaw Pact continue to sustain huge nuclear and conventional forces. Their respective military forces no longer reflect the real security threat.

An October 1987 poll asked Americans whether they regarded the Soviet Union as the central threat to 'our way of life.' Nearly half, 48 per cent, cited economic troubles within the United States as the greatest threat; 31 per cent named terrorism from Third World countries and extremist groups; and only 17 per cent said that the military threat within Europe, from the Soviet Union, was the greatest of the three threats mentioned.[5]

Several objective forces are driving our societies towards the same conclusion that the public has already expressed about the East–West confrontation. Shrinking demographic pools in Europe are going to make it harder to sustain the troop levels we have seen in the past. This is true for both the NATO and the Warsaw Pact countries. Most NATO countries have declining birth rates at this time, with the exception of Turkey. Another objective force that seems to be working is the economic constraints that I have already mentioned which make the task of keeping the troop and armour levels constant relatively more burdensome. Thirdly, of course, Gorbachev's initiatives have gone a long way to convince the Europeans, and perhaps to a less extent the Americans, that Soviet intentions in Europe are no longer primarily military. Given the convergence of these factors, the new conventional arms control talks, referred to as the Conventional Stability Talks, may avoid many of the pitfalls that dogged the MBFR talks from 1973 until their unfortunate conclusion.

A third 'snapshot' reflected in American opinion, one not altogether consistent with the other things I have mentioned, is that there is a substantial imbalance of conventional forces in Europe. Unfortunately, the American public now believes what they have been told for four decades: that the Warsaw Pact has a decisive advantage over NATO forces. I do not particularly share that view, at least not in its simplistic formulation, and nor do many knowledgeable experts in the field. Bean-counting exercises can identify simple numerical imbalances, of course; we all know that. But these simple totals do not necessarily have strategic or military validity and, frankly, I believe there has been a systematic over-stating of the Soviet threat for various political and budgetary reasons. By a number of measures, NATO is actually ahead of the Warsaw Pact. Most people would rather be on NATO's side than that of the Warsaw Pact if hostilities broke out.

A couple of items in that regard: NATO has spent more on defence than the Warsaw Pact every year since 1976. To speak of a steady twelve years of spending on NATO's side exceeding that of the Warsaw Pact is obviously misleading, because personnel and other costs are not comparable. The figure does represent, however, an indicator of commitment.

Another item. Including the forces of France and Spain, NATO has more active ground forces (about 2.4 million) in the area covered by the Conventional Stability Talks than the Warsaw Pact countries (approximately 2.3 million). It is a fact which I think has not yet been absorbed by public opinion.

Another item. It is generally agreed that NATO has a larger number of major surface navy combatants, battleships, cruisers, destroyers, etc. as well as overwhelming technological, if not quantitative, superiority in combat tactical aircraft.

Finally, although the Warsaw Pact is credited with greater numbers of tanks globally, along the critical Central Front the ratio is only 1.4:1. This is not particularly good for the attacking side which must begin hostilities with a substantial advantage. Furthermore, NATO tanks are generally newer, of a more recent vintage.

So in summary, NATO has important advantages in weapons technology training in readiness and reliability, certainly of its members as well as in logistical support. This is not a perception which is normally shared by the American public.

It does, however, highlight two dangers inherent in the public having this view. First, if we can't agree on the conventional balance among ourselves, it will be difficult to formulate a negotiating position in the up and coming conventional arms control talks. Gorbachev has shown himself to be an effective negotiator—we can expect him to put forward proposals that will be appealing and NATO will be well-advised not to be caught unawares or without sensible proposals of its own.

The second cost of this public misconception also relates to these negotiations. If we give the Soviet Union credit for having a certain number of tanks or personnel, it can claim significant concessions by making what might actually be relatively modest reductions. The Soviet Union may well offer asymmetrical reductions based on NATO force assumptions. It could make the Soviet offer appear more generous than it really is. How will we explain our rejection of these offers, particularly given Gorbachev's skill in public relations and our own statements of Soviet strength? This leads to the conclusion that we must look very closely at the data issue. We have a deep-rooted tendency to assume the best about the capacities of our adversaries and the worst about our own capacities. In conventional arms talks this could prove disastrous.

My final observation is that Americans have a strong and deep distrust of nuclear dependence. Witness the apparent popularity of President Reagan's SDI. While it has been attacked by more thoughtful observers, nonetheless it has a popular life of its own which lives on because of a deep abiding American distrust of dependence on nuclear weapons. Another illustration of this claim is the almost universal popularity of the INF proposals.

For years, the United States has been deploying nuclear weapons in Europe to symbolise its commitment to European security. These weapons provided 'more bang for the buck' and, since they were American weapons, they were intended to ensure that a nuclear war would escalate from a conflict in Europe to a global exchange. In this way, American security was tied inseparably to the security of Europe.

This has been called into question over the last few years by the Euro-missile crisis. Nuclear weapons can no longer 'reassure' our allies, as witnessed by the enormous difficulty in placing the Pershing II and Cruise missiles in the Netherlands and Belgium. Both in critical quarters in Europe and the United States, the deployment of these weapons prior to the INF agreement was seen more as a threat to security than as a safeguard.

Today, NATO has some important decisions to make about its nuclear posture. The INF Treaty embodied the double zero option by removing both medium and long-range INF weapons as we all know. NATO is now deciding what it wants to do about a possible third zero option—namely short-range nuclear weapons. Will the Alliance negotiate away these weapons or will it attempt to modernise them? Those options are diametrically opposed.

A new modernisation debate would probably create a domestic Euro-missile political crisis for at least some of the countries involved. The other question NATO must face in terms of its nuclear posture is whether it will continue to rely on the first-use of nuclear weapons to deter a conventional attack. If so, it would have to continue to deploy tactical nuclear weapons near the frontline in a 'use them or lose them' posture.

Let me conclude on the note that the challenge to leaders of the United States and the NATO countries is to understand public opinion as well as to shape it, preferably constructively. Public opinion represents a legitimate concern in many cases, while in others it exposes real dilemmas and contradictions, even unresolved choices, particularly in terms of burden sharing. Given the economic constraints which the United States and its allies will increasingly face, we will all have to take greater note of public perceptions in the future.

Sources

1. Marttila & Kiley, Inc., Americans Talk Security, *National Survey No. 4*, April 1988, p. 55.
2. The Daniel Yankelovich Group, Americans Talk Security, *National Survey No. 3*, March 1988, p. 83.
3. Mellman and Lazarus Research, *Defining American Strength*, Results of a survey of American voters conducted for the World Policy Institute, October 1987, p. 14.
4. *Ibid.*, p. 5.
5. *Ibid.*, p. 12.

PART 3

Sharing the Costs of Global Security

CHAPTER 5

American Globalism in the 1990s: The Prospect of Increasing Power and Declining Influence

WALTER GOLDSTEIN

There is a cynical and yet realistic rule operating in international affairs. It holds that régimes of both the right and the left will be tempted to pursue elusive chimera, hate symbols and crusading metaphors in place of serious goals of foreign policy. Hard-headed critics, from Bismarck to Henry Kissinger, have warned against the delusions which guide diplomacy in the most liberal or the most reactionary of states. American diplomacy in particular has been accused of running races with its own wilful misconceptions, whether in Vietnam or in shoring up global deployments. Many allies and adversaries have been found guilty too of chasing phantom policy goals.

The conflict between symbolism and reality was especially disturbing in the upheavals just before and after the Second World War. Ideology and imagery impelled the powerful struggles of the 1930s and the 1950s. Today the trend is again becoming critical. It is said that the structure of order is moving from a bipolar to a multipolar distribution of power; and that the nuclear condominium of the superpowers is beginning to erode. What will become of their fabled 'hegemony' and their lambent authority, it is asked, if their collective security alliances should start to unravel? Will they maintain their symbolic status or their pre-eminence if threats of nuclear war should recede; and for how long can a superpower sustain its leadership image if its economic growth falters, or if it should fail to match the wealth gathering skills of its allies and trade competitors?

These questions have been disregarded by the Bush Administration for two good reasons. First, it has fared poorly in competing with the peace bandwagon driven by Mikhail Gorbachev. Recent opinion polls taken in America and Europe have shown large majorities favouring Gorbachev over Bush in the peace race; 84 per cent of West Germans responded that

Russia posed little threat to their security.[1] Second, Bush has not yet projected his own style of policy leadership.

Following after the eight flamboyant years of Ronald Reagan, he has yet to capture the leadership of the American political system and the emotional loyalties of the Western Allies. He has to counter the economic challenge offered by Japan or the political jousting of Gorbachev. Assuming moreover that he will stay in the White House until 1997, he must also begin to shape up a strategy to take America into the next century.

A surprising note has appeared recently in the execution of United States foreign policy. The country-by-country components of American diplomacy have rarely fitted together as well as in the last few years. Although no great breakthrough has been scored by American policy makers, neither are any terrible crises impending. Levels of tension have receded for the time being in Central America, the Middle East, and elsewhere in the Third World. A pragmatic policy of coping with troubles one at a time has brought quiet, if not peace, to the world order. Hence the Bush Administration is fearful of moving too fast in negotiations over arms control, NATO security, or new openings with Eastern Europe and China. It does not want to imperil the current lull in world affairs with premature questions. The next century will start soon enough. There is no point in worrying now about the policy metaphors which American leaders will have to invent if the era of superpower confrontation should move to an unexpected close.

George Bush has revealed a personal style which shrinks from risk and political speculation. His Administration is led by men clad in conventional wisdom and Cold War pieties. He has been strangely unsure of himself in facing the ex-enemy in the Kremlin, fearing that President Gorbachev will outwit him or deny him access to the hostility symbols which once served him well.

It used to be profitable to draw on the Kremlin as an image of threat when it came to passing the defence budget or rallying reluctant allies. Now he has to cope with a smiling adversary who preaches peace and who offers a flood of concessions—real or imaginary—on prime television. If Bush has to abandon his cosmology of global struggle it could be debilitating. Rousing metaphors of 'the free world' endangered and of 'manifest destiny' rampant had helped turn back the communist threat. Today they could only hinder the adjustment of popular expectations to the post cold war era.

There has been a marked transformation in public opinion at home and overseas since Reagan left the White House. Gorbachev has seized political advantage with allusions to the reunification of Germany and the disarming of Europe. He talks warmly of a 'common European house' in a demilitarised world. The belief has spread among America's allies that the Cold War confrontation (as Mrs Thatcher put it) is drawing to a close; and that the Soviet future is not what it used to be. Clearly, the United States must respond. It cannot stick with the alarms and war cries of the past. If it is to engage the East bloc in a constructive dialogue in the Bush years it must move beyond military doctrines of containment.

The speeches given by Bush since entering office have been cautious but upbeat. He argues that the United States economy has expanded for seven years without a break and that America has been fortified as never before by its costly military build-up (on which it spent $2,000 billion since 1982). While the communist economies steadily deteriorated, America added significantly to its GNP at home and its influence overseas.

Bush dismissed the criticisms of the day—that the Federal budget was badly overdrawn, that military spending was excessive, and that the external deficit costs a fortune in interest servicing. (It now stands at $500 billion or 10 per cent of GNP and it could double in just a few years.) He believes that minor corrections will remove these faults without pain; and that the American century is certainly not coming to a close. His confidence impressed millions of voters in the 1988 elections. He succeeded too in deflecting attention from the debate waged in the elite press over the presumed course of America's 'historic decline'.[2]

Bush has to overcome two great obstacles. First, his election victory failed to bring him a popular mandate or a charismatic image. He had tried to improve his own image and the Republicans' minority position in the Congress, but to no avail. In fact, he was the first President in 200 years to enter office with *both* the House and the Senate held more firmly than before by the opposition. Constitutionally it is expected that pitched battles will be fought between the Chief Executive and the Congress. Thomas Jefferson assumed they would provide high drama and low politics; the Watergate and Iran–Contra investigations fulfilled the worst expectations. Bush's fight with Congress appears each night on the television evening news as theatre of great excitement. But he has won few of the skirmishes.

Second, it is difficult for Bush to win acceptance for his foreign policy initiatives. His predecessor had brought about the recovery of the economy and of America's global influence without paying for it. Reagan had lifted the national debt in eight years from $1,000 billion to $2,800 billion, and he ran up a deficit in external trade that will not be removed in this century. By common consent, the resort to deficit financing can go no further. The nation's strength has been built on debt and a reliance on foreign borrowing. As the first order of business, Bush has been obliged to rescue the nation from drowning in red ink. Until he can rebuild the resource base of the Government and the economy he cannot hope to define his own foreign policy.[3]

The Resource Base of the Bush Administration

Since his first days in office, Bush has had to make an awesome choice. Should he abide by the Gramm-Rudman schedule for budget retrenchment—that had been widely hailed and never implemented—and slash government outlays by at least $50 billion a year; or should he repudiate the schedule and fight Congress for every cent over the next four years? So far he has chosen both routes. He has co-operated with Congress as far as possible, bargaining over line item cuts in the $300 billion bill for defence and the $450 billion for social welfare transfers. But he has refused to raise tax revenues to shorten the deficit, leaving a grave fiscal problem to be fixed by the Democrat majorities in both Houses. The evasion has infuriated the Democrats. They might yet retaliate, as the Constitution allows, by denying his Administration the appropriations it needs to restructure the nation's foreign commitments and defence outlays.

Three sets of resource calculations must be decided by Bush. Each will generate intense political debate. The first concerns the use of fiscal deficits, the second looks to tightening monetary policy, and the third to cuts in defence. If any of them are handled ineptly, the Bush team will fare badly in the 1990 and 1992 elections and the nation will forfeit the dynamic momentum which Reagan had bought.

FISCAL POLICY

Economic growth in the 1980s was boosted by an unhealthy surge in consumption and imports. Manufacturing investment and R&D funding declined steeply, export markets were lost and the spending spree bounded forward. As a result, the average debt of each family doubled and the total indebtedness of the public and private sectors climbed to $9,400 billion.[4] Now two dangers are looming near. The heated pace of growth has begun to strain the system; with 95 per cent of the workforce employed, and plant capacity almost fully used, there could be a quick upturn in both inflation and interest rates. Strikingly, there is also a fear of recession. If the Federal Reserve Bank should push too hard to throttle the supply of money and credit, it could shore up the dollar but at the expense of choking off growth. Across town, the White House wants to expand business activity (and tax revenues) by relaxing fiscal and monetary restraints. The dispute has troubled the Stock Market and Congress and it has led to an erratic trading range for the dollar.[5]

To the optimists, the prospects look bright. They believe Bush's assurance that the country can literally grow its way out of debt. They cheerfully expect that the deficits in the Federal budget and in the external accounts will linger for years to come, and that additional debts will have to be listed too: first, the bail out of 2,000 troubled Savings and Loan Banks and the repair of leakages in nuclear reactor sites will cost $150 billion or more; second, the $170 billion servicing of the debt will balloon if interest rates should rise, possibly driving the national debt from $3,000 billion to $12,000 billion in the 1990s. Meanwhile, net domestic savings have fallen to an all time low of 2 per cent of GNP. Since the Federal deficit absorbs the same portion of GNP as household savings, foreign loans are relied upon to pay both for business investment and the excess of consumption.

This prospect feeds the pessimists' worst anxieties. On some days, they force stock and bond prices down, if business looks too vigorous or the dollar too strong. On others, they relent, predicting that a 'soft landing' of GNP growth will avoid the dangers of *both* inflation and recession. But their fear remains: that GNP growth cannot, in one fell swoop, cure the economy's structural ailments, boost exports, balance the federal budget and curb inflation. Their chief worry is that if taxes are not raised, interest rates will soar. That could stifle business activity and investment at home and export earnings overseas. It could also hurt Third World governments that are desperate to reschedule their vast debt obligations to the International Monetary Fund and to the United States' banks.[6]

MONETARY POLICY

A second resource calculation concerns the money supply and the dollar. If the United States currency appreciates, American exports could be hurt and the European Monetary System would have to impose painful adjustments on the British and French currency. Alternatively, if the dollar should fall, Japanese and Asian creditors will be reluctant to buy Treasury bills and the European Community might stiffen the protectionist measures built into the 1992 package of legislation for a single European market.

Conceivably, if the dollar remains unstable, the United States will forfeit power in the tough bargaining sessions of the Group of Seven finance ministers when they try to modify currency exchange rates and national monetary policies. In round numbers, the dollar had surged 50 per cent upwards between 1983–85, 50 per cent downward in 1987, and then 15 per cent up again in 1989. If this volatility is not controlled, and if nothing is done to curb the United States deficits, the Group of Seven might have to assert itself. It could either force an exchange correction or create a new currency unit divorced from the dollar. Such an imposition would not be welcomed by a nation trying to assert its authority as the banker of last resort and the policeman of world commerce.[7]

The merchandise trade deficit runs to $150 billion a year and the shortfall could realistically top $3,500 billion (or 32 per cent of GNP) by 1999.[8] If oil prices and import bills keep rising, along with interest payments on the deficit, the shortfall will have to be financed by foreign creditors and by the sale of domestic assets at absurdly low prices. Foreign holdings of United States cash assets currently total $1,500 billion; and another $300 billion worth of factories, farms and skyscrapers has been acquired by overseas purchasers—using cheap dollars. The sale of profitable American companies to pay for consumption and imports is not wise. Massive claims stand against American financial reserves, and sovereign control of many industrial and capital assets could be surrendered.[9]

DEFENCE SPENDING

The third calculation turns to placing limits on funds for national security. Nearly 27 per cent of the budget and 7 per cent of GNP goes to the Armed Services but their spending has not kept pace with four years of inflation. In Fiscal Year 1988 the Joint Chiefs of Staff asked for an increment of 5 per cent above the rate of inflation. Since this would have lifted their budget from $300 to $400 billion a year by 1993, Reagan kept them only to 2 per cent. Now even this figure cannot be met.

Congress has already cut 3 per cent from the Pentagon as the Gramm-Rudman plan required. But the reduction is still not enough. Unless taxes are raised or domestic outlays shrink by $50 billion a year, the military Services will have to bear much larger sacrifices. That will lead to a firefight among their powerful allies on Congressional committees and in the defence industries. It could hurt a President who is trying to build both a political support base and a new strategy.

For a start, the Air Force has lobbied aggressively to keep buying the expensive B-1 and B-2 bombers, the MX and the Midgetman missiles, and the Strategic Defense Initiative (or 'Star Wars' as it is derisively known). The Navy pleads for its fleet of 600 ships, including nuclear submarines and 15 aircraft carrier groups. And the Army clamours for additions to its armoured and infantry division strength. Ironically, the missions and force levels needed in the 1990s have not been lucidly defined, only their cost and manpower ceilings.

Each of the Services has pressed for increments of pay and benefits to maintain the all-volunteer Army and for funds to buy spare parts, ammunition, and training. Too much of the $2,000 billion build-up in the 1980s went to pork barrel or long-term weapons contracts, leaving operations and maintenance under funded. Half a million American troops (out of a two million total) are stationed overseas and they take half the Pentagon's budget. A full funding of their operational and combat readiness could topple the balance of payments.

The International Power Equation

A set of tentative projections can suggest some of the shifts in the power balance that might emerge in the 1990s. The projections point to the diplomatic options which might be available to the United States. Three clear trends in the emerging power equation can be noted:

(1) the lowering of threat levels in the world order,

(2) the mounting rivalry among America's allies and trade competitors, and

(3) the changing behaviour of America's adversaries.

THE EASING OF THE THREAT

If both superpowers have to curb their force structures, military conflicts will become limited to the smaller nations at the periphery of the world order. Even if the superpowers' 'stand-off' is stable, their skill in conflict management will be sternly tested. Naturally, their policing of regional conflicts or arms control treaties will not go unchallenged. Powerful groups in NATO, Washington or Moscow might try to block disarmament plans, though their capacity to stir up crises will probably be curbed. Optimistically, future summit meetings might aim for new goals—to reunify Germany, or extend the nuclear non-proliferation and test-ban treaties. Or the superpowers might at last tackle the worst of the dangers, the threat posed by high technology terrorism and missile warfare in the Third World.

THE INTENSITY OF RIVALRY

The superpowers have conceded that Third World crises can no longer be met with unilateral displays of force. If regional security is to be guaranteed, they must rely on economic assistance or joint diplomatic efforts rather than direct intervention. In such regions as the Middle East, where the authority of the superpowers runs thin, it is impossible to insert mobile deployment units or unilateral peace missions. Again, when it comes to settling debts or trade disputes, America cannot force its way alone. If it ever strong-armed Panama or Iran it would be challenged by its allies and trading rivals. Some might go so far as to revoke the banking or commercial treaties that bind the richer nations together. Others might seek to change NATO rules if they resented the pursuit of United States interests.

THE BEHAVIOUR OF ADVERSARIES

It now appears that the effects of *perestroika* will be revolutionary and possibly irreversible. But what will happen to Soviet policy if Gorbachev should fall and his enemies replace him with hard-line cadres? Should American aid be extended to help him hold on to his position, and should it also go to the foundering communist régimes in China and Eastern Europe? It is hoped that they will turn to America rather than to Western allies or the Soviet Union for aid and protection. The hope is not shared by irate conservatives and Congressmen who still view communist régimes of any stripe as belligerent adversaries.

What will become of the less developed countries (the LDCs) in this conservative new world? Theorists claim that recent wars have been limited, small in scale, and short in duration because the bi-polar power structure constrained all challengers. If it ever weakened, wars would escalate beyond control. A similar theory holds that if the global economic structure should tremble or falter, financial chaos would ensue—bringing in its wake upheavals of inflation, debt repudiation and bloody civic strife. Preventive action must be taken to defuse the debt time-bomb, it is warned. It must be launched by the IMF and international banking syndicates, and not by the Wall Street banks or the United States Marines.

For example, Argentina is contending with an inflation rate of 12,000 per cent and Peru of 5,000 per cent. Their neighbours have cut real wages sharply and half the people live below the poverty level. The region is ripe for revolution but there is little that outsiders can do. Unilateral bail-out plans for the LDCs in dire straits are simply not feasible. Nor are various invasion plans to stabilise chaotic areas—as Israel found in occupying Beirut. The only hope is for United Nations peace-keeping teams to monitor a cease-fire and for United States forces to stay out.

Gorbachev has suggested that the Soviet Union is no longer interested in fomenting world revolution and that United States peace-keeping functions should be powerfully extended. But no one in the Bush Administration believes that the last has been seen of Soviet incursions in Third World conflicts; or that the United Nations will be able to impose peaceful solutions in complex trouble spots. Conversely, neither is anyone sure that America's days as a global policeman and bank manager are ending. A sizeable part of the defence effort still goes to deployments in the Third World, and the United States Treasury follows a Lone Ranger role in dealing with LDC debts. The habit of acting alone is hard to break. Bush has played the sheriff at the IMF or the OAS. His policy in Nicaragua ignored friendly neighbours and the OAS, and sternly warned the Soviets to stay out. Over trade fights in OECD and GATT brawls he plays the role of honest policeman enforcing the law.

It is assumed that the greatest promise of the 1990s will appear at the summit level and not at the periphery. The INF Treaty (1987) and the Conventional Forces in Europe (CFE) agreement have already lowered tensions and distrust between the superpowers. Soviet television cameras filmed their Joint Chiefs of Staff entering the secret war room in the Pentagon. Teams from the West filmed the disputed ABM radar installation at Krasnoyarsk and the protest rallies held in Moscow and the Baltic states— and the massacre in Beijing. Even though belief in détente is so popular, Cold War doctrines still hold the military planners tightly in thrall on both sides.

What caused the turn to détente? Was reasonableness brought to the Kremlin by the disrepair of the communist economies and their political systems? Or were they scared by the American threat to send them into a ruinous arms race, as Reagan once argued? A more credible explanation is that *both* superpowers found the Cold War far too expensive and unprofitable, as did their leading allies. Defeat in Vietnam and Afghanistan, and in the no-win arms races of the 1980s, was daunting. Yet both kept adding to their forces, though the goal of military 'superiority' lay beyond reach.

The weapons race survives because strategic doctrine is rigidly hinged to the axioms of the 1950s—to containment, protracted war fighting, and nuclear deterrence. Doctrine helps justify the purchase of additional strategic bombers, ICBM missiles, ABM defence systems, and modernised arsenals for conventional war. Though the Strategic Arms Reduction Talks (START) envisage 50 per cent reductions over the long term in offensive nuclear forces, there will be no sharp lowering of the guard and no sudden agreement to phase out ICBMs, SDI, or conventional defences, especially in Central Europe. NATO insists that it must guard against Soviet adventurism or any resort to military tactics to solve political crises; and no one in Washington urges the withdrawal of American garrisons or the decoupling of NATO's forces from the United States strategic deterrent. Negotiations over START and forces in Europe (CFE) will have to move slowly and cautiously, if only to control the rise of peace expectations.

Mr Gorbachev scored a diplomatic coup when he offered to withdraw 500,000 troops and 10,000 tanks; he also proposed to cut the Soviet defence budget, and to pull down the Berlin Wall. He even admitted that the Warsaw Pact held an advantage over NATO in force levels and that disproportional cuts might be arranged. Bush responded with a four point disarmament plan of his own. But he gained a greater success by advancing a timely compromise to bring the warring members of NATO together. He skilfully played off the British and West German arguments over arms control by approaching each with token concessions. This allayed the suspicion that United States leaders would not be able to keep NATO intact if the Soviet peace offensive ever accelerated. But it did little for the smaller European nations in NATO, many of whom refuse to pay higher military costs or to station nuclear weapons on their soil.

A change in the power balance is long overdue. Two massed armies have faced each other for forty years, jointly deploying five million troops and 12,000 combat aircraft. They are back-stopped by 25,000 tactical and strategic warheads of each superpower. Yet the entire structure cannot cope with real world problems, such as the technology gap in European industry or the fragmenting of régimes in the Eastern bloc. It may be that the superpowers' garrisons will have to stay in place for another forty years—to deter violent change in the *status quo*, to anchor the two Germanies to their present moorings, or to impose a successor régime on their continental allies. For nearly two generations, they have managed to 'buy hegemony on the cheap', exchanging an umbrella protection against nuclear war in return for the political deterrence paid by their restless allies. But can this strange Faustian bargain last out the century?[10]

Rivalries and the Displacement of Threats

The new Soviet leadership has managed to dispel the ogre image which had been developed by Stalin and Brezhnev. President Gorbachev began to dismantle Western suspicions, first by removing the Soviet Army from Afghanistan—after it had been defeated—and then by offering to withdraw the SS-20 and SS-4 missiles from Europe. These surprise offers broke the logjam that had blocked East-West relations since détente negotiations had failed in the 1970s. Gorbachev then threw in a third card, the proposal to reduce deployments and eventually to reunify Europe. His talk of a 'common house' was warmly received in Europe. It also sowed more discord in NATO than the anti-nuclear marchers had achieved during years of protests against the American 'occupation forces' and their nuclear planning for a flexible response strategy.

Politically, there was not much that the United States could do to ease the domestic arguments or to promote the wealth of its fretful allies. Its own GNP growth lagged behind the European Community (EC) and East Asian average by 2 to 3 per cent a year. Over ten or more years, as Paul Kennedy has demonstrated, that could lead to a serious loss of export markets, industrial technology and capital accumulation.[11] Japan and West Germany, especially, had gained a competitive edge in accumulating industrial R&D and high-tech exports. They had built energetic trading states which outclassed the warfare régimes that the nuclear giants had created with debt. Export revenues accounted for 54 per cent of the West German GNP, while Japan's surplus surpassed the sum of OPEC's earnings at the zenith of its power.[12]

American voters became irritated by the profit-seeking of their allies. They saw Asian and European companies selling high-tech equipment to the Soviet military that compromised United States defence secrets. The earlier row within NATO over the Europeans' contributions to the Yamal natural gas pipeline and grain sales to the Soviet Union had eventually subsided. But resentments resurfaced when American firms were denied entry into markets in the Eastern bloc while EC exporters rushed in to sell. More than 50,000 United States troops were garrisoned in South Korea, Taiwan and Japan, but each of them closed up their markets to American exports and each totted up a large surplus on the United States trade flow. Yet it was America which, in fact had to borrow from them to defend their end of 'the Western world'.

It would be an exaggeration to say that isolationism had seeped back into American politics but there was a mounting bitterness. It was directed against America's friends and competitors rather than against its established enemy. Few of them acknowledged the stand which the United States had taken on their behalf. Traditional allies had been too free with criticism of United States action in Grenada, Libya, Israel and Nicaragua. They had even objected to the American handling of an issue from which they benefited, the withdrawal of Soviet troops and INF weapons from Europe. Some had attempted to cut separate deals with Gorbachev and his colleagues, though few were successful. To critics in Washington, they were rudely barging into the fast lane of summit traffic bound for Moscow.

There was one matter that rankled above all, the 'free rider' issue: too many allies had failed to pay their fair portion for the common defence. Burdensharing within the alliance was unfair. The nations enjoying the largest trade surpluses are among the most miserly. The average expenditure on defence was roughly 3 per cent of GNP in Europe and 1 per cent in Japan, but it was close to 7 per cent in the United States. In very rough terms, *per capita* military expenditures were $100 a year in Japan, $440 in Britain and $1,225 in the United States.[13]

It was widely believed that the United States' contribution to NATO security topped $150 billion a year, while the other members of NATO (who are collectively richer) paid only $100 billion. The exact figures have never been agreed as methods of budget accounting vary, especially in Japan. Although Japan paid only part of its security costs, its defence bill (in fully appreciated yen) was $40 billion, the third largest in the world.[14] It also offsets some of the payments for the United States units (at $45,000 per soldier per year) which guard its naval and air lanes. Japan's trade surplus worldwide is $90 billion, most of it earned in the United States. The Japanese now ask how much more aid must they give to help the dollar and the United States trade balance; and how much more will the United States exact as a political price for the protection of its allies?

The assessment of the Soviet economic position is nearly as troublesome. Russia's real growth halted a decade ago and it now reports a steep rise in inflation and in the deficit (two non-Marxist terms which have acquired wide currency). Both the deficit and the defence budget place twice the burden on GNP that is seen in the United States economy, and their export revenues are inadequate. The rouble is inflated 15 times over the black market rate and military spending is obviously excessive. It appears that Soviet leaders have begun to read Western statistics and that they have decided, too, to revise the cost/benefit calculus of Cold War expenditures.

The prospect which hurts in Washington is that of losing a valued enemy. If Russia is reduced to the status of being just another dissatisfied power, albeit one with a massive nuclear arsenal, it should no more be treated as a privileged opponent than should China. Why was it allowed to co-sponsor a Middle East summit conference, for example, if it could no longer 'deliver' the Arabs whom it had expensively armed? And why should negotiations with the struggling régimes in Warsaw and Budapest have to be approved in Moscow? The customary answer was that the Soviet Union alone possessed a superpower capacity for meddling and destruction. But if its economy is so battered and the Soviet republics are seething with subversive ethnic passions—along with the fragile régimes in the rest of the Eastern bloc—then they should forfeit their prize status in the superpower condominium.

Adversaries, Real and Symbolic

The objectives of American foreign policy had once been explicit. There had been a world class enemy to overcome and no expense was spared in creating containment perimeters or sophisticated deterrence systems to defend the 'Free World'. As a side benefit of founding a protective alliance, American idealism had sponsored campaigns to promote human rights and market values. But first a firm bulwark had to be built—to deter communist encroachments and revolutions, to face down any attempt at nuclear blackmail, and to anchor the Western alliance. Then, as a shrewd afterthought of the Marshall Plan, American economic interests would expand into markets overseas.

The formula worked well for an entire generation. It held the assaults of Stalin and Brezhnev at bay. Over time, Soviet trouble-stirring was either blocked or exhausted—depending on which version of history was to be believed. One conflict after another spread across the Third World but Soviet restraint was relatively constant. Numerous upsets occurred among LDCs and client states but Americans learned to predict Soviet responses—until Gorbachev arrived.

For its own part, there was one good reason why the United States managed to fulfil its global role, even after its budgetary and trade deficits had soared out of control. Its rivals in Europe and Japan were absorbed in regional rather than global security issues. There was no secure bridge or alliance to link them together except through the United States. It alone provided the symbol of a nuclear umbrella and the reality of prime export markets, and the dollar served them all as a reserve currency. For the Soviet Union, American policy was of supreme military and political concern. For Japan and the EC, like it or not, American management capability determined their economic welfare and their lasting security.

What is likely to happen in the 1990s if rivalry comes to replace hostility as the *modus operandi* of international activity? There is much talk of America's 'historic decline' but none of its rivals will match or surpass its pre-eminent position. Admittedly, many of the East Asian economies are expanding rapidly. The concentration of trade in the Pacific could take wealth away from the post-industrial societies on either side of the Atlantic. If the EC manages to integrate its political and economic resources after 1992 it could overtake America in aggregate GNP—but not *per capita* wealth. But will Europe and America spend enough on high-tech industries, R&D programmes, and science training to hold on to their lead in the multinational race of banks and exporters?

For the last twenty years, the Atlantic nations have made too few investments in their high value-added industries, in information services and in public education. They have fallen back in the contest to upgrade productivity and export trade.

Their multinational firms have moved assembly plant to cheap wage nations overseas, taking valuable jobs, R&D patents, and capital with them. The manufacture of electronic products, computer components and automobile parts can be shifted over-night to Taiwan or Mexico. The workforce in the older Atlantic cities could, therefore, find themselves on the losing edge of the international division of labour—with their high wage jobs in peril. If the faster moving of the LDCs continue to prosper they will pick up the wealth which the laggards forfeit. The losers will have to reduce their standards of living and subsist on credits advanced by the surplus nations.

Violence and revolution among the LDCs are likely to spread but they will not extend Cold War confrontations into the hot tropics. Wars will surely involve client states but they will not be seen as surrogates for Superpower contests. Bloody coups and ethnic strife will sweep across all too many of the LDCs. Unfortunately, reformist plans—such as the Brady scheme to reschedule debt—will not be helpful. Most of the debtors are too poor and some are starving. With $1,300 billion outstanding, interest on the debt brings a rich flow of funds from the poor to the rich. American bank and trade interests could be damaged if the capital flow ever stopped.

Like Reagan, Bush is more interested in dealing with former adversaries than with the debt-ridden and anti-capitalist régimes of the Third World. This is short sighted. Forty per cent of United States exports and enormous bank loans depend on the LDCs' solvency. If a wave of inflationary crises or defaults on debt servicing swept through the LDCs, the American balance of payments would be badly impaired. Obviously, neither a military invasion nor a massive loan bail-out can be launched in case a major debtor begins to collapse—whether in the Philippines or in Brazil. But it is time for American leaders and other Group of Seven nations to start planning for likely disasters.

Style and Symbols in the Bush Years

What will be the character of foreign policy in the Bush term? The first emphasis will be on caution. After every activist President leaves office there has been an interlude for policy retrenchment.[15] Bush has replaced the Reagan style of summit pageantry and activist rhetoric with an approach which he calls '*status quo* plus'. His advisers, including Jim Baker at the State Department, Richard Cheney at the Department of Defense, and Brent Scowcroft at the National Security Council, are cautious men who shun bold initiatives even on great occasions. This was shown at NATO's 40th anniversary, at the Group of Seven summit in Paris, and on the visit to Eastern Europe. If there is a Bush doctrine, it will eschew the brash phrases and deficit funding of Reaganomics.

Caution may be Bush's first axiom, but 'stand back' may be the second. The term does not imply disengagement or disinterest; just a 'kinder and gentler' loosening of commitments. Support for Nicaragua's dubious freedom fighters has already been phased out and Angola's will be the next to go. A few air and naval squadrons will be sent home from the Gulf and East Asia, but the 520,000 troops garrisoned in South Korea and NATO will not be disturbed. They need not be lavishly equipped. After all, their task is chiefly to stand guard over strategies formed in the 1950s—when imminent war was expected rather than a lasting and uneasy peace.

The 'stand back' strategy will be implemented piecemeal and in constant consultation with the Allies or Congress—depending on which is the more influential. SDI will not be scrapped without a loss of face in the Congress or at the summit but its $5 billion a year funds have been heavily cut and more will go once a deal can be struck with its critics. Funds for the MX and Midgetman land-based ICBMs will also be slowed down, the B-2 bomber will be replaced with airborne cruise missiles, and one aircraft carrier group will be cancelled.

These changes will be marginal at best. Current force structures will be preserved, either to placate the Congress and the Armed Services or to bargain with contentious allies. No matter how it is concealed, the push for retrenchment will take precedence over any Grand Design of strategy. The NATO doctrines of 'flexible response' and forward deployment will, therefore, remain unchanged; budgets will be stretched out; and the Allies will be consulted before any changes are made.

If Bush settles for 'stand back' solutions to larger military problems, he will find no easy way out on economic matters. The clamour for trade protection already poses a threat. He might yet face a bloodier fight with Congressional trade lobbyists than with NATO allies or export competitors. The trade surplus countries are becoming wary of investing in United States assets or securities because Bush has not modified his monetary or fiscal policies. He has used the Super 301 clause of the Omnibus Trade Act to scare nations offending against free trade (as the United States understands it), but he might have to sign protectionist measures. He will give way on some tariff bills before Congress if bigger battles have to be fought over the American deficit or trade rules in Brussels and Tokyo.

Reagan had used popular support and borrowed funds to rule grandly. Bush cannot sustain the political dynamism or the budgetary chicanery. He must attend to the mismatch between America's global commitments and its limited national assets if he is to write credible policy plans for the 1990s. So far he has not begun. Perhaps he never will.

At the turn of the next century the United States economy will still be stronger than that of the EC nations or Japan and richer than it is today. But it will not be strong enough for America to act as an independent agent. Its adversaries will surely enjoy less respect than its industrial and financial rivals. And the chances are that its nuclear lead will not be challenged, and that its military might will go unmatched. The reality of its power, as measured by its high-tech industry and arsenals, will be impressive. Yet its autonomy as a superpower will fade unless Bush revises his present values.

This projection is based upon five or six optimistic assumptions: that there will be no major war or exercise in nuclear blackmail; that an international debt crisis or an explosion of inflation can be controlled; that there will be no serious proliferation of nuclear weapons, chemical warfare or missile launching capabilities in the Third World and that no wave of revolutionary upsets will disturb the world order. If this future works, the best outcome may be for the Soviet economy and the nuclear duopoly to survive the century intact.

Yet even if the threat of nuclear conflict recedes there could still be ruinous trade wars and financial landslides. The world trade system is burdened with a surplus capacity of manpower, raw materials and manufactured products. A shift in the international division of labour could enrich the newly industrialising countries (the NICs) and penalise the older, richer economies which are too sluggish to modernise. The locus of productive wealth and export income has already shifted from the Atlantic coasts to the Pacific rim. Further moves could lead to serious trade disputes, labour hardships, and economic dislocation. If it cannot control these events America's status as a superpower will be sadly diminished.

It would be unwise to write off the US power position as a spent force. A quick turnaround of policy priorities could bring about major corrections. For a start, an increase of only 3 per cent in tax rates could close the deficit and rally the dollar. Similarly, a marginal shift in the tax code, to reward savings and restrict consumption, could raise vital business investment and repair the balance of payments. A reduction of $50 billion in defence procurements each year (adding up to $500 billion in the 1990s) would lop off interest payments. Further, if new international institutions were created, the flow of speculative capital and free trade could be firmly regulated. That would lay a terrible spectre to rest: the fear that a momentous clash of industrial or currency policy will create more hardship and devastation than a world war.

It is assumed that the Soviet Union and China will stay whole, though in a less powerful condition; and that America's allies and rivals will contest any attempts to regain its hegemonial influence. But what is worrying is that the international system will be highly vulnerable to trade warfare.

Aggressiveness will increase if there is a glut in the supply of primary com-
modities, unskilled labour, and manufactured exports. In that event, the
dollar on its own cannot be relied on to stabilise a global system fraught
with tensions, tariff manipulations and financial speculation.

Bush talks in imagery about restoring balance to the system, but he cannot achieve it with conventional means of foreign policy or economics. In
the resource conflicts of the future, deficit financing and living on credit
will not be easy to sustain. They could lead to an overburdening of the
system and a loss of the symbolic authority of the state.

Bush has summoned the spirit of American pragmatism and free market
beliefs to restore a favourable equilibrium in the worldwide correlation of
military and market forces. It is the charge of the United States to lead the
'free world' to this metaphor for fulfilment. Yet this is the flaw in his
approach. He used patriotic images cleverly at election time but now they
must be replaced with the complex realities of policy choice. Though
abstractions of national security and economic logic are more attractive to
him than the calculus of hard data, the time has come to put them aside.

If President Bush is to plan a fresh foreign policy he must substitute
empirical calculation for patriotic slogans. Tough choices must be made
regarding budget priorities and retrenchment tactics. So far he has taken
no serious action, preferring transactions of imagery, as one might expect,
to the hard data of monetary strategy and fiscal change. But his lead time
for action is limited. The clock is running against him. If he stays with the
symbolism of policy goals and ignores their real world costs, the debate over
America's 'historic decline' will run indecisively through the 1990s.

Notes

1. On the shift in American public opinion, see Daniel Yankelovich and Richard Smoke
   'America's New Thinking', *Foreign Affairs*, Fall 1988, Vol. 67, No. 1, pp. 1–17. For
   opinion polls in Europe, *The New York Times*, May 16, 1989.
2. For an optimistic analysis of the US recovery, see Samuel P Huntington 'The US—
   Decline or Renewal', *Foreign Affairs*, Winter 1988/89, Vol. 67, No. 2, pp. 76–96.
3. A book on the policy dilemmas facing the Bush administration has been recently
   published by C Fred Bergsten *American in the World Economy*. Washington DC: Institute
   for International Economics, 1988.
4. Much of the economic data cited below comes from the *1988 Annual Report* of the
   Federal Reserve Bank of New York.
5. Current fiscal and monetary options are clearly reviewed by James Schlesinger
   'Domestic Policies and International Capital Flows', in Martin Feldstein, ed., *The United
   States in the World Economy*. Chicago: University of Chicago, 1988.
6. For an extensive analysis see Walter Goldstein 'The Continuing World Debt Crisis', *International Tax and Business Lawyer*, Summer 1985, Vol. 3, No. 1, pp. 119–153.
7. A critique of monetary policy appears in Benjamin J Friedman *Day of Reckoning*. New
   York: Random House, 1988.
8. See the *1988 Annual Report* at Note 4 above.
9. For a popular exposé on the sale of US assets, see Martin and Susan Tolchin *Buying Into
   America*. New York: Times Books, 1988. For statistical data, see 'Foreign Direct Investment in the US', *Survey of Current Business*, August 1988, Vol. 68, No. 8, p. 69–ff.

10. A good critique of US foreign policy in Europe and in economic affairs has been written by David P Calleo *Beyond American Hegemony*. New York: Basic Books, 1987.
11. The classic source for literature on 'America's decline' is Paul Kennedy *The Rise and Fall of the Great Powers*. New York: Random House, 1988. See pp. 467–469.
12. Perceptive comments on world trade tensions appear in Thorold Masefield 'Co-prosperity and co-security: managing the developed world', *International Affairs*, Winter 1988/89, Vol. 65, No. 1, pp. 1–14.
13. The calculation of NATO defence expenditures and the discrepancy in national accounting procedures appear in *The Military Balance 1987–88*. London: International Institute for Strategic Studies, 1987.
14. Provocative data and interpretation appear in Michael Mansfield 'The US and Japan: Sharing Our Destinies', *Foreign Affairs*, Spring 1989, Vol. 68, No. 2, pp. 3–15.
15. See Walter LaFeber *The American Age*. New York: Norton 1989.

CHAPTER 6

Sharing the Costs of Global Security

MICHAEL BRENNER

The United States is experiencing a transformation in its foreign relations. The world environment in which it reached superpower status is being altered in some fundamental respects. American recognition of stricter limits on its capacity to shape international affairs is leading to a re-examination of strategic ends and means. This process touches all aspects of America's external relations—including its most basic security ties.

Prominent among the altered features of the global landscape is the appearance of serious structural weaknesses in the United States' economic position. Not always separable from other, political transformations, the loss of economic paramountcy is the anxious point of reference for the present reappraisal of the nation's world role. This reappraisal cannot avoid having implications for America's position as protective ally and leader of the Atlantic Alliance. For the conditions that fostered the growth of American power and influence in the post-war era are inextricably tied to the historic forging of the Atlantic partnership. While the belief in shared interests and sense of common destiny are strongly rooted, there is reason to wonder how the currents now running in the broad sweep of America's global relations will affect the shape of its engagement in Europe and the precise forms of its commitment to the North Atlantic Treaty Organization.

There are certain givens that can help anchor our analysis of where and how economics is going to impinge on alliance relations. There is, first, the elementary truth that the post-war period saw the United States enjoy at once economic pre-eminence and political predominance. We are all familiar with the image of an America that bestrode the world like a colossus: its immense industrial system that provisioned the Grand Alliance intact and unchallenged; the dynamic expansion of American business into the four corners of the globe; and the coronation of the dollar as the world's *de facto* money. This great economic engine provided the credits, goods and markets for the reconstruction of Western Europe. It also instilled the self-confidence in American economic invulnerability that permitted the enlightened efforts in support of the European Community (and the revival of Japan). Moreover, economic internationalism went hand-in-hand with Washington's willingness to assume wide responsibilities for the security of friends and trading partners.

There is no presumption here of an economic causal primacy in the explanation of why the United States discarded its traditional isolationism and committed itself to both formal alliances and a policy of diplomatic activism. The salient point is that American internationalism is linked in people's minds with American economic strength; this is true for Americans and allies alike. This belief is a compound of three notions:

- that an economically strong America has the resources to commit to defence and security needs;
- that an economically strong America is more inclined to take an enlightened, internationalist view of its interests; and
- that an economically strong America is a more effective leader.

American activism on the economic front, in support of an open world economy and as custodian of the principles of collective management on which it is built, is associated with a willingness and ability to engage American military power abroad on an equally enlightened basis. There is the further assumption that economic and security assets are fungible to some extent. Not only does economics provide the means for building and projecting military power, but itself can be used as an instrument for exerting power (as well as for defence against the pressures or blandishments of others). Equally, a strong security position built around stable alliances encourages constructive policies that augment economic strength.

The first of these several linkages has received the most attention, deservedly so. The United States' exceptional wealth undoubtedly has made it easier for America to shoulder a heavier defence burden than its principal allies. Economic strength and a popular sense of well-being obviates the need to make unwelcome trade-offs either between defence expenditure and domestic spending *or* between non-specific defence expenditures and outlays in support of NATO specific commitments. Conversely, a sense of economic vulnerability and weakness promises grating budget fights along with a more sceptical look at overseas commitments.

America's purported economic decline is now so much a staple of discourse about alliance futures that we are inclined to accept it as truth while debating its significance. In order to assess properly the consequences of shifting economic conditions, it behoves us to determine more precisely just what has happened.

The American Economic 'Decline'

The issue of America's purported economic decline is expressed in three questions:

- is the United States today, and in the near future, in an inferior economic position than it was a decade or so ago?; and if so, to what degree?
- what is the nature of the decline and what are its principal causes?
- what are the likely effects, direct and indirect, on its alliance relationships?

Economic decline connotes two things—first, diminished economic strength measured by the static indicators of GNP growth, employment, and price stability, and second, a deteriorating position in the world economy: competitiveness in world markets (as reflected in trade balances), the value of its currency, and debt situation. Generally speaking, the former refers to a country's absolute economic condition and performance; the latter reflects relative position which, in turn, can be expected to affect strongly absolute conditions in the future. What do the numbers tell us?

Looking at the first set of indicators, the picture is reasonably bright. The American economy in the 1980s has grown at a commendable rate of 3.4 per cent. It has outperformed the EEC countries as a whole, by a clear margin, and has an even wider edge over the Federal Republic of Germany. Among the major OECD economies, the United States lags only the Japanese—by a substantial margin (*Sources: OECD; Bundesbank*). Steady growth has been accompanied by an employment boom, with unemployment (as of 1988) at a fifteen-year low. Inflation has been kept in check on the whole although running at a markedly higher rate than in the Federal Republic and Japan, its two main trading and financial rivals.

On the surface, then, it would seem that the United States is generating ample economic resources to cover the country's outstanding defence obligations. Defence spending (which peaked in real terms, in 1985 at the height of the Reagan military build-up) has subsided to the point where it represents 6.0 per cent of GNP. By comparison, throughout the 1960s, military expenditures amounted to more than 8 per cent of GNP. During the past decade, it never reached a figure higher than 6.8 per cent of GNP. Of this total, roughly a third is earmarked for NATO forces (or 2.2 per cent of GNP). The comparable figures for the major European Allies are: United Kingdom—5.5 per cent, FRG—3.3 per cent, France—4 per cent, Italy—2.2 per cent (*Source: IISS*).

These figures could be viewed even more optimistically when we bear in mind the diminished threat to American security interests in the Pacific and East Asia. It does not unduly strain the facts of the situation to judge the threat level there to be at its lowest point since the 1920s. The overriding strategic reality for the past decade has been the silent partnership among the United States, Japan and the People's Republic of China in a tacit alliance to maintain the political *status quo* and to block the spread of Soviet influence. It has been animated as well by a common economic interest in encouraging continued growth in what has become the most economically dynamic region of the globe. While the evolution of this strategic configuration has not been matched by a commensurate reduction in American defence commitments, one can foresee some decline in military resource requirements.

The United States' economic condition then can be assessed rather favourably insofar as the resource/military commitment balance is concerned. A more searching examination of the broader economic situation though yields a less optimistic conclusion. It derives from two features of the economic environment: loss of competitiveness in world markets; and, more distressing, serious structural defects in the American economy whose current prosperity has been achieved in large part by borrowing on the future. They are closely related.

The *budget deficit* has drained resources from an already thin capital pool to pay for current consumption. Thereby it has crimped investment in the basic structure of the economy. A net inflow of funds from abroad has been required to meet the borrowing needs of the Federal Government, and of American business. A large fraction of that influx represents the recycling back into the United States of the dollar *outflow* produced by a string of record *trade deficits*. In consequence, the United States is now the world's biggest debtor nation—having substituted borrowed cash for the ownership of real assets.[1]

From this sombre economic perspective, one can foresee profound and potentially grave implications for the United States' ability to play the role of world leader, the meeting of alliance obligations foremost among them. The numbers tell much of the story themselves. Debt is at the heart of the matter.

Between 1981 and 1987, the outstanding obligations of the United States Government rose from about $1,000 billion to $2,800 billion, nearly tripling Federal indebtedness. Since the beginning of the decade, the Federal deficit has averaged 4.2 per cent of United States' national income. (By 1988 it was down to 2.4 per cent.) The figure of 4.2 per cent comes close to matching the rise in federal spending as a fraction of GNP between 1979 and 1986 from 20.5 per cent to 23.6 per cent—without a parallel increase in revenue.

The budget deficits take on heightened significance when reviewed together with the equally large balance of trade deficits. The two are causally inter-related; and they are given their full significance when examined together. The trade deficit grew dramatically through the mid-1980s before dropping modestly and then levelling off toward the end of the decade. For the period as a whole, the United States' import bill exceeded the value of its exports by a remarkable $900 billion. The causes are multiple—not least among them being a badly over-valued dollar which crippled American export industries while exposing the domestic market to the cheaper products of foreign competitors (until the Louvre and Plaza accords began to bring it down in 1985). The high dollar exchange rate, in turn, was due largely to the high interest rates which the Treasury had to offer in order to attract from abroad the funds needed to meet its heavy borrowing requirements.

This degree of fiscal imbalance is not in itself exceptionally high as a fraction of GNP. The US deficit is lower than in Canada, less than one-third of Italy's, and marginally higher than in France. What makes it so damaging to the nation's economic future is the United States' extraordinarily *low savings rate*. The American economy (individuals and businesses) saves only 5.7 per cent of national income. This compares unfavourably to a savings rate of over 12 per cent in the FRG, and an astonishing 16 per cent in Japan (*Source: IMF*). Indeed, the United States on this score is close to the bottom of the league table among OECD countries (*Source: OECD*). A shortage of domestic capital explains, in good part, the faltering rate of investment in new industrial plant and equipment—which now represents a smaller share of national income than at any time in the post-war period, *and* the lag in funds devoted to civilian research and development (at a post-war low).

These investment rates augur poorly for future economic performance, and already are contributory causes of the difficulty American industry has faced in trying to maintain a competitive position in markets at home and abroad. The erosion in that position has been evident in the large balance of trade deficits that have been on a scale comparable to the budget deficits.

The United States paid for its merchandise imbalance with an outflow of dollars. Given the greenback's special place in the world's monetary system (serving as a reserve asset, and transaction currency) they were accepted as settlement on accounts. A substantial portion of these dollars find their way back to the United States in the form of credits and investments. This reverse flow permits the United States to (1) satisfy its capital needs unmet by domestic savings; and (2) to finance its domestic budget deficit as foreign dollar-holders have been purchasing approximately 40 per cent of the securities issued by the US Treasury.

The process has helped to stabilise both the budget deficit and the overall balance-of-payments, *but* at the cost of a dramatic reversal in the United States' position in world finance. In the span of a decade, America went from being the world's largest creditor nation to becoming its largest debtor. By the end of 1988, the United States' external debt amounted to approximately $500 billion. If projections prove correct, the figure will reach $1,000 billion by 1992 (at which time the twin deficits will have been brought into balance—or so it is hoped); since the United States will need to attract an additional $500 billion of foreign capital to cover its current account deficit *and* to meet its borrowing needs. By that time, the United States' ratio of net foreign debt to national income will be about 15 per cent, a level on a par with that of some developing countries (*Source: IMF*).

The Consequences: Economic

The direct economic effects of American indebtedness can be spelled out with relative ease; the policy implications can also be identified—if with less precision. One conclusion to be drawn from this data is that real national income will stagnate (or, at best, increase slightly) for the balance of the century as the United States must devote between 1 per cent and 1.5 per cent of its annual GNP to repay its foreign creditors.

Servicing the debt will require a merchandise trade surplus of roughly $70 billion a year—which represents a turnaround of $190 billion from the 'improved' trade performance at the end of 1988. In effect, that means a wealth transfer from the United States to foreigners that is likely to depress incomes at home. Assuming an annual growth rate of 2.5–3.0 per cent, and taking account of population increase, the average American family will find its standard of living rising marginally, if at all. America will not be poorer in absolute terms. However, it can be expected to slip further behind such high-flyers as Japan while doing less well than most of its other allies. The one possible saving grace is that foreign creditors will reinvest in the American economy the interest received on outstanding investments and repayments of principle. Were it to happen, more robust growth rates might be expected even as an increasing fraction of national economic assets falls into the hands of foreign owners—an eventuality likely to give impetus to economic nationalism in the United States.

The United States could be slated for a period of low growth anyway. As external debt mounts (the precise rate of growth depending on what progress is made in bringing down the budget deficit), it probably will become harder to attract foreign capital. Interest rates will have to rise, with a predictable dampening effect on economic activity. Hence the resources earmarked to pay off existing obligations would be extracted from a sluggish economy.

In this sense, the United States will have lost some considerable control over national economic policy. The judgements that foreign investors make about the attractiveness of American securities, and the creditworthiness of American borrowers, cannot fail to exert a major influence on monetary decisions and, in the long-run, on fiscal policy too. In an even more striking way, the ever present risk of a flight from the dollar—with its potential for unsettling the American economy—could force the hands of America's leaders when confronted with key decisions. The proximate source of the pressure would be the markets *and* the governments of creditor countries— above all, Japan and the FRG. Their enormous stake in American solvency— outstanding loans, world monetary stability, and their growing ownership of tangible assets in the United States—will overcome their shyness about acting the role of creditor.

The second unavoidable economic consequence is that budget constraint will be a constant feature of the policy environment. The imperative to bring the budget into balance is undeniable. Mounting financial pressures may force populist sentiments to yield to prudence in allowing for some tax increase. The resulting augmentation of revenues notwithstanding, belt-tightening will be the name of the budgetary game well into the 1990s. Defence will be called upon to contribute at least its proportional share of the new austerity. It already has. Military spending began to decline in real terms in 1986 while its share of GNP dropped from 6.8 per cent to 6.0 per cent. Furthermore, the Bush administration has acknowledged that over the next three years a total of $300 billion will have to be cut from the Pentagon budget as originally planned by President Reagan—and that projection is based on optimistic forecasts of economic conditions and budgetary politics.

Defence spending is vulnerable to budget-cutting pressures on a number of counts. Reagan's $2,000 billion military build-up is widely seen as having yielded less in real military capability than that huge sum led one to reasonably expect. More defence for the dollar is now both the common objective and the basis for justifying holding military spending in check. The much publicised instances of waste in managing the Pentagon's resources, along with the shocking string of procurement scandals, has left its mark in an increasingly sceptical public opinion and austerity-minded politicians.

Consequences: Political

In general terms, it is not hard to discern what this pattern impends for the United States' engagements in NATO. The issue of burden sharing within the Alliance, more specifically the costs of maintaining American forces in Europe, will certainly be in the spotlight and will be in for careful scrutiny for a number of reasons. In strictly numerical terms, it is tempting to make the facile correspondence between that portion of the defence budget dedicated to NATO (by rough calculations 30–35 per cent of the overall Pentagon expenditures, or 2 per cent of GNP) and the overall budget deficit (2.4 per cent of GNP).

Similar arbitrary statistical couplings relate America's external payments for maintaining forces in the European theatre with the trade deficit. While it may be faulty logic to read a causal relationship into a correlation of facts, those looking for arguments to reduce the United States' military presence in Europe and/or looking for politically acceptable ways to shrink the budget deficit will find these juxtapositions convenient and appealing.*

The linkage between the United States' trade problems, in particular, and its alliance obligations will be a staple of future debates about the

---

*It is noteworthy that public opinion in the United States remains firmly in support of maintaining the current level of military commitment to NATO—70 per cent by one survey. An even higher percentage of those queried, 82 per cent, oppose the withdrawal of American troops from the European continent. (*Chicago Council for Foreign Relations, 1987*.)

desirable and affordable level of American military presence in Europe (and East Asia for that matter). For it is true that the United States has run large balance-of-trade deficits with two countries that figure prominently in the reappraisal of defence commitments and burdens: Japan and the Federal Republic of Germany. The $60 billion trade deficit with Japan (1987) and the $30 billion trade deficit with Europe (1987) are roughly equivalent to the direct expenditures made on behalf of European and East Asian defence. (Although the troubling question of America's evolving strategic relationship with a Japan of burgeoning economic strength lies beyond the scope of this paper, I believe it fair to say that the growing irritation Americans feel about the sharing of benefits and costs with the Japanese might well sour attitudes toward allies and trade partners across the board.)

This simple (and perhaps simplistic) point was made repeatedly by Representative Gephardt (the new House majority leader) during the 1988 Presidential primaries; in his oft-quoted words,

> today we maintain a global defence financed with dollars borrowed from creditors who are the very countries we protect.

Gephardt's particular brand of mercantalist isolationism is not sweeping the United States; but these sentiments are being echoed by a growing faction within Congress. In 1988, a special House Armed Services subcommittee passed a resolution calling for a 'long-overdue realignment of defense responsibilities' in the interest of equity and as required to ease America's economic burdens. The committee bluntly called upon the allies to 'share or pay for all the additional costs incurred by the United States in stationing its forces overseas.' Even so sober and sympathetic a legislator as Senator Sam Nunn has argued the case that 'our allies have to do more' in the light of the exigent financial situation.

An even more revealing sign of things to come under the Administration of George Bush was the declaration of senior officials that allies should shoulder more of the military and financial burden for the common defence. In a report issued during the transition, they stated their conviction that 'a more equitable sharing of the roles, risks and responsibilities for the common defence is needed and is achievable.' Cast in diplomatic language, the Allies had not been making 'significant contributions relative to their ability to contribute.' The unmistakable implication was that the United States would try to change that situation.

Budgetary considerations were a contributory factor to President Bush's proposal in June 1989 to cut back American Forces in Europe by over 30,000 men. It was a central point in the policy response to Mikhail Gorbachev's bold call for sharp reductions in both conventional and tactical nuclear forces. A domestic economic consideration thus impinged on the evaluation of sensitive security issues; while, at the same time, the prospect of major arms accords could be used to blunt arguments about the excessive costs of maintaining American troops in Europe.

There are other, less tangible connections between these economic trends and America's alliance role that give reason for apprehension. In the past, the United States' leadership in the security field was matched by its economic leadership. The convergence no longer exists. For the foreseeable future, America's economic viability, indeed its solvency, will depend on financial infusions from abroad. The unavoidable result will be a diminution of the United States' authority and influence in the monetary sphere, and across the gamut of economic issues and institutions as well. What had been a slow, incremental adjustment from American supremacy to the exercise of leadership as *primus inter pares* has now begun to turn into a dramatic role reversal. Direction from Washington on what is needed to maintain the health of the collective economic enterprise has begun to lose credibility and persuasiveness. Furthermore, Washington now is hearing the importuning voice of America's creditors as to what is necessary to put its financial house in order—for the good of the United States and of the world economy both.

An important American voice, of course, will continue to be heard on all matters of collective economic management. After all, the United States remains the largest economy in the world, and by virtue of that fact alone the most important. It therefore is not surprising that Robert Camdessus, Managing Director of the IMF, should declare that the number one need for the world economy is that 'the United States reduces its budget deficit substantially.' Nonetheless, moral authority on economic issues is being transferred along with financial power from the United States to its partners, eroding America's leadership position in the process.

An equally serious concomitant is the aforementioned loss of American autonomy over domestic financial and monetary policy. For all intents and purposes, those policies now must pass muster in Tokyo and Bonn. However discreet they, and other economic partners, might be about the offering of counsel, there cannot fail to be a measure of discomfort—and even some unpleasantness, as this new relationship unfolds. It is a cause for concern. There is little in the American historical experience, certainly not in this century, of being judged by other nations—nations whose governments are in a position to act on those judgements in ways that affect directly and immediately the well-being of the United States. One cannot help but raise the question of what, in the final analysis, will be the effect on American self-confidence, and on the United States' readiness to continue the burdens and responsibilities of leadership in the security field.

Consequences: Security

A number of points suggest themselves for consideration in any attempt to answer that question. First, there will be a disposition in some political and economic circles within the United States to cite the costs of the country's military establishment (and especially its expenditures in support of allies) as the cause of the United States' economic decline. At the very least, outlays for meeting the United States' security commitments will play a part in the political discourse on how to make ends meet. There is already evidence of this tendency in the reception accorded Paul Kennedy's much-heralded book, *The Rise and Fall of the Great Powers*.[2] The evocative term 'imperial overreach' has attained a level of usage that enshrines it in the political lexicon. There is something captivating about the notion that were the United States to lighten the burdens it has borne as world guardian of the peace, the release of economic resources soon would restore American competitiveness, increase savings, ease the budget deficit, and scale back external debt.[3]

A word of caution though. It is not a world view that has been universally accepted; certainly not among foreign policy élites in Washington. Not only have the proponents of 'imperial overreach' exaggerated the importance of defence spending's contribution to the deficit crises, but their advocacy of a retrenchment from present alliance commitments runs counter to the still durable consensus on the proposition that alliance engagements are essential to the protection of basic American national interests. This viewpoint has been succinctly stated by one of Kennedy's critics who accuses him of urging 'the United States to risk unhinging the delicate balance of its alliances to increase marginally the resources available for the domestic economy.'[4] We should remind ourselves, however, that the level of support which the 'Kennedy position' eventually gathers will depend in large measure on the progress made in bringing the United States out of its economic difficulties.

The issue, as is so often the case, is one of perceptions of reality as much as it is one of objective facts themselves. The hard economic realities point in two, somewhat divergent, directions. Adequate resources to fund America's global security commitments do exist, by some reasonable standard. Equally, there has been a role reversal in the United States' external economic relations associated with its new status as a debtor nation. *So the proper question is not whether America, like Britain a generation ago, will get so threadbare that world power seems too expensive a luxury. Rather, it is whether the United States can muster the will and determination to put its economic house in order while making the adjustment in the range and character of its leadership appropriate to its changed circumstances.*

A second proposition to be considered in an appraisal of what portends for the United States' alliance future is that the appeal of a postulated reversion from foreign obligations and commitments is likely to register more forcefully among the populace at large than among government officials. The compelling truths of life in today's interdependent world are, for understandable reasons, more strongly felt by those with the responsibility for conducting the nation's affairs. The exercise of power in this case will act as an antidote to emotions of disappointment and frustration as Washington contends with a world in which interests remain relatively constant while the resources for satisfying them shrink.

Perhaps an accurate depiction of the national mood at this juncture in American history would describe it as self-absorbed and distracted rather than isolationist in the traditional mode. The much cited resurgence of American national pride during the Reagan years has restored some of the internationalist sentiment dissolved during the painful post-Vietnam recessional (as survey evidence indicates). But the damage done to American self-confidence has never been fully repaired. If this means greater risk aversion, less willingness to engage American military force in ventures of dubious need or merit and a disinclination to view every world issue through the optic of an East/West conflict universal in its proportions, most of those concerned about the reliability of America as an ally would say: 'so much the better'. However, if the enduring after-effect of the Vietnam experience is to leave the American political psyche tender and somewhat fragile, the implications might not be all to the good.

A wavering national self-confidence is now being shaken by the embarrassments of declining economic potency. No nation likes being outclassed or surpassed; surely not in ways that are transparently evident. It is an especially irksome experience for a country whose collective identity is so closely bound up with a deeply ingrained sense of its exceptionality and superiority. It threatens a reversion to the kind of parochial and introverted nationalism which both conforms to American historical experience and permits the preservation of its singularity. One rationalisation for such a 'drawing-in' could be that an ungrateful world is not worth a strenuous American effort to protect it *nor* the economic sacrifice that it seems to demand. Political insularity is a natural companion to economic insularity; retrenchment in both areas promises relief from the relentless (and in part self-imposed) pressures of proving oneself before allies whose stinting praise for your protection is accompanied by what appears to be a penchant for bending the rules on economic matters.

The picture that I have drawn is not offered as a prediction of the shape that the collective public mood will take—much less policy. Rather, it is presented as a description of latent tendencies which could crystallise in this form under foreseeable economic circumstances. Whether, and to what extent, it does so will depend upon a number of variables, including the type of leadership exercised by the Bush presidency and the wisdom shown by America's allies as they too come to terms with some unwelcome new realities. All the same, we should recognise that the state of national feeling in the United States is one factor that will influence and constrain how government leaders in the Western democracies work their way through the conditions we have been discussing.

As a final remark on this point, it is worth reminding ourselves that the Congress is normally the more sensitive barometer of the public mood than is the executive. It long ago discovered superconductivity—of the political kind. When, and if, that mood expresses itself in a pronounced neo-protectionist and/or neo-isolationist manner, it could exacerbate pre-existing tensions between the White House and Capitol Hill on issues such as burden sharing *or* add additional obstacles to joint efforts at finding a politically acceptable solution to the problem.

Alliance Relations

What of inter-governmental relations themselves between the United States and its European allies? Our analysis might benefit from distinguishing the broad trends that we might expect in the way the Alliance conducts its affairs from possible changes in the structure of the relationship itself. The former points to the 'atmospherics' of the Alliance; the latter covers more basic matters of Alliance commitments, strategy and forces. Looking at the former area first, a number of ideas present themselves for our consideration.

It is unreasonable to expect issues of economic diplomacy to be kept entirely separate from security issues. I am referring here not only to the objective reality whereby the question of resource availability and allocation impinges on defence spending and force deployments. Beyond that obvious connection, one can expect that the disposition of parties to what will be pressing economic matters on the Atlantic (and Pacific) economic agenda will colour attitudes toward security matters and affect how they are handled.

For one thing, America's authority has been undermined by its reckless handling of its financial affairs. This cannot fail to diminish its capacity to exert leadership in the Alliance (especially in the light of the Reykjavik near-debacle, and the Irangate embarrassment). Credibility is not something that can be easily compartmentalised issue-area by issue-area. Indeed, the very fact that the United States has for so long been the firm hand on the tiller that kept the Western military-cum-economic enterprise on a sure course means that its faltering grip is all the more unsettling.

There is no gainsaying the fact that there are going to be some disagreeable moments when America's creditors have to play Dutch uncle to their outsized financial dependent. The depth and complexity of the economic predicament, as well as the awkward role reversal, pretty well ensures as much. So at a time when NATO will be addressing profound issues concerning the fate of the Alliance and its design for dealing with a rapidly evolving Soviet Union—all of which requires delicate handling and trust—relations between Europe and America are likely to be bedevilled by an irritating string of clashes on tangential matters.

Deft and discreet handling of these predictable economic contretemps could go a long way toward minimising the deleterious effects on alliance solidarity and collaboration. *Whether* it will be forthcoming depends in large measure on a return to sobriety in American economic policy, itself hostage to the compulsions and vagaries of domestic politics. The more difficult challenge, though, may be faced by the United States' European partners. For the forthcoming role reversal in the financial realm places on them a singular responsibility: namely, fashioning policies that take account of the misfeasances and nonfeasances of the titular leader and largest member of the alliance.

In the past, it was American policy that was the secure mooring for the Europeans, on economic as well as security matters. It was Washington that customarily counselled against neglecting collective needs and interests while government wrestled with national concerns. Allies and trading partners, for the most part, felt they had done their duty when government decisions on domestic policies were made prudently and with disciplined regard for common interests. *Now, and in the near future, conditions require not just that they conduct their affairs responsibly. They also must do things necessary to compensate for the errors, omissions or indiscipline of the United States.* At times, it will mean deviating from what one might regard as the right and proper course.

An illustration is Bonn's response to pressures to keep interest rates lower, and economic growth somewhat faster than its own cautionary instinct about inflation dictates. The FRG has been called upon to do so out of fear that too restrained a policy would deny the United States the export markets it needs to reduce its trade deficit and could trigger a flight from the dollar unless Washington pushed up its own interest rates to a level that threatened serious deflation. Bonn is understandably frustrated since this choice between virtue and necessity presents itself because of continued fiscal irresponsibility in Washington. It will not be the last time that a European partner of the United States will find itself in such a predicament.

The implications for security relationships are identifiable. There is above all the aforementioned question of *credibility*. In the light of America's apparent imprudent behaviour in the economic sphere, can the United States be counted on to act responsibly on matters of more direct concern to NATO? Is the weakness and vacillation of American political leadership in confronting the public with the hard truth about economic choices a harbinger of how it will cope with the inevitable pressures to scale back American troop levels beyond what conforms to the requirement of ongoing disarmament diplomacy. More generally, what will the Alliance mechanisms for forging consensus look like in the future were America's leadership capability shown to be hampered, if not irreparably impaired, by its less than brave management of its own economic problems? That would be no small loss.

It is difficult to overstate the value to the Atlantic Alliance of American leadership. The United States' catalytic role in NATO's founding aside, Washington's leadership has been essential to the Alliance's stability and achievement. For a grouping of states that organises itself to achieve a set of collective purposes, the tasks of building consensus and defining a common strategy (not to speak of a common plan to deal diplomatically with a common foe) is significantly facilitated by the presence of a paramount government. As leader of the Alliance, the United States customarily has set the agenda; kept the organisation clearly focused on the common interest; absorbed costs in the common good; and undertaken commitments out of duty, not just convenience (Washington's initiative in the dispatch of a multilateral naval task-force to the Persian Gulf is a recent, not uncharacteristic, example—albeit in an out-of-area situation).

This is not to say that the United States always has been a ceaseless fount of enlightenment and selfless behaviour; nor is there an implication that her allies have been habitually shortsighted and self-interested. Rather, the point is that NATO with an acknowledged leader has a greater ability to sustain common enterprises than it is likely to have without such a leader. The logic of any alliance's internal dynamics supports this judgment; so too does the experience of how American strength and seeming invulnerability enable it to lead the Atlantic Alliance.

Specific Effects

Our outline of the changes in the tenor of Alliance relations expected to flow from adverse economic conditions has made only passing allusion to specific security issues. It is possible, though, to discern what some of these concrete effects are likely to be and to indicate how the shift in 'atmospherics' will influence attempts at preventing problems and/or resolving them. There are four whose importance deserves mention.

1. A Drawdown of US Forces? Most obvious is the question of American force levels in Europe; or, to put it plainly, the economically motivated inclination to pull out a fraction of the five-and-a-half army divisions now in West Germany. Proposals along these lines have surfaced periodically during the past twenty-five years, so it is understandable that the postulated danger is seen by some as yet another case of crying wolf. In this instance, the wolf may very well be at the door. While the preponderant view among Washington officials still opposes such withdrawals, certain aspects of the situation are different from the past.

Above all, the seriousness of the United States' financial problem is without precedent. Not only are budget-cutting pressures now a fixture of the policy environment, but attention is sharply focused on those presumed causes—the trade deficit and the mounting foreign debt—that bring to the forefront the outlays made to maintain American forces overseas. Moreover, as we noted earlier, the easy juxtaposition of these expenditures with the growing financial dependency on allies/trading partners tightens the connection in the minds of the public and policy-makers.

Another factor that makes this crisis over troop levels different from its predecessors is the undeniable easing of the military threat that in the past has chilled the Alliance into keeping its military guard up. In the wake of President Gorbachev's dramatic announcements at the United Nations in December of 1988, of substantial reductions in the Red Army, much of the scepticism about the Soviet Union's declared intention to reach an historic accommodation with the West is dissolving. Whatever uncertainties attach to the long-term prospects for enduring détente, there is a pervasive sense of a qualitative change in the threat whose existence has been the Atlantic Alliance's *raison d'être*.

The coincidence of these historic developments in the Soviet Union with an economically induced reappraisal of Alliance responsibilities is at once fortuitous (it removes some of the urgency, and dread, about the intra-alliance adjustment process) and disconcerting (it raises fear of an exaggerated reaction to the Soviet démarche as a reformulation of need, too conveniently defining part of the problem out of existence). Logically, one way to cope with a relative decline in power is to reduce the threat through diplomacy. It would follow that Washington should be most eager to take Soviet intentions at face value. In fact, optimism waxes most strongly among some of the European Allies; e.g. West Germany, Holland, Denmark (at least insofar as attentive publics are concerned).

This apparent paradox carries the risk of aggravated tensions within the Alliance, as surfaced in the spring of 1989. Then, Washington was seen as pressing its European allies to maintain levels of conventional defence expenditure *and* to modernise tactical nuclear forces at the same time as it was urging a go-slow on meeting Gorbachev's attractive proposals for conventional disarmament and the triple nuclear option. That situation proved so untenable as to force President Bush to reverse himself by bringing forward his own ambitious disarmament plans.

2. Burden Sharing? A move to increase the contribution of the European Allies would be a natural complement to any contemplated reduction of American forces in Europe. It too is a classic method of compensating for a dominant nation's relative power decline. The detailed discussions of comparative costs and burdens will continue along the course they have taken for years. Does the fact that the European members of NATO provide 60 per cent of the active forces and 80 per cent of the reserves offset the greater overall American defence outlays?; what weight does one place on the fact that European defence spending has grown faster than that of the United States since 1985?; if the United States feels constrained by its budget deficits to reduce its forces, why not cut home-based troop levels rather than NATO forces?, and so on.

It would not be surprising to see more intense haggling over procurement practices, standardisation of equipment, and logistics—even in the more relaxed environment created by the optimistic talks with the Soviet Union on conventional force reduction and stabilisation. All these issues have dollar signs attached to them that will glow all the brighter as austerity thinking takes a tighter grip on Washington policy-makers (and as the Allies brace themselves for a bout of American arm-twisting). These hardy perennials of intra-Alliance policy-making are likely to be weighted with greater political meaning in an atmosphere made tense by the omnipresent American economic crisis and the pressure to relieve the United States of financial burdens. The debate on cost-sharing will be linked once more tightly to the problem of economic adjustment.

3. Technical Fixes: The perceived imperative to generate more military power at less expense can be expected to reinvigorate ideas for using new weapons systems based on advanced technologies as a partial substitute for, or supplement to standard conventional forces. This line of thinking was sketched for us by the team of veteran American officials and defence intellectuals who authored the 1987 study on *Discriminate Deterrence.*[5] The report's rather baroque structure discourages careful reading. The effort required is worth the investment however. For its core thoughts express another trend of thinking that will influence official policies and security decisions over the next several years.

The penchant for exploiting the West's technological advantages to strengthen its military posture and to reinforce deterrence is nothing new; indeed, it has been a trademark of American strategic thought since the 1950s. (That was the era in which Henry Kissinger, one of the panel's members, came to prominence with his daring proposal to build NATO defence—as well as deterrence—around mobile, self-contained nuclear-armed units designed for war-fighting missions.) The report's technological optimism is almost palpable as it declares 'the Alliance's posture could be transformed by new military technologies.' What is noteworthy about this statement is that its recommendations are explicitly offered as a solution to two of NATO's outstanding problems: how to offset a prospective shortfall in NATO manpower (whether for demographic reasons or because of a cut-back in American troops); and how to strengthen the credibility of the Alliance's deterrent function in the wake of the removal of medium range nuclear missiles brought about by the INF treaty.

This is not the place for a detailed analysis of the group's proposals, or the premises on which they are based. The point to be made here is that the push in this direction is encouraged by the widespread scepticism about troop levels. The narrowing of options for strengthening conventional forces, due to economic constraints, can be expected to heighten interest in technological solutions.

There is a nuclear dimension to this debate. It has been posed succinctly by Samuel Huntington (another participant in the Discriminate Deterrence project):

> Budget-cutting logic means [we] should build up nuclear forces, arms control logic means [we] should build up conventional forces.[6]

Throughout NATO's history nuclear weapons have been given more prominent attention whenever doubts arise about the capabilities of conventional forces. It follows that any reduction of conventional forces associated with an American strategy of retrenchment would prompt interest in new concepts for incorporating nuclear weapons into Alliance force planning. Whether that connection still holds is singularly difficult to assess on this occasion given counter influences; *inter alia* the INF accord, Western Europe's 'nuclear allergy'—accentuated by Gorbachev's triple zero proposals, and generally by a lowered sense of threat from the East. All that can be said with confidence is that if, and when, a retrenchment of American forces occurs, it will colour perceptions of all issues related to the United States' commitment to European defence and its credibility.

4. Strategic Arms Negotiations. The larger European voice on Alliance matters will surely be accompanied by more direct involvement in strategic arms talks as well. The string of arms control negotiations between the superpowers, which have become a contrapuntal theme to the Cold War, has been largely a Soviet–American affair—despite their implications for the security of America's European allies. Consultation within the Alliance has been part of the process; and in the past few years it has grown more extensive as the links between the INF and the START talks were established. Characteristically, though, *strategic arms negotiations* have been bilateral encounters. In the future, they will have to follow a different mode—for three reasons.

Objectively, the intersection between the strategic plane and the regional, or tactical, plane (encompassing conventional as well as nuclear forces) is so unmistakable that progress at one level depends on a satisfactory management of interests at the other. Politically, the European Allies have been increasingly sensitised to the risk inherent in a segmental approach, especially under conditions where public opinion is narrowing the space they have for adjustment and compensation based solely on strategic military considerations. Furthermore, as the Europeans assume a larger, more independent role *vis-à-vis* the United States (on conventional forces, or theatre forces and in Alliance planning) they will be less inclined to defer to Washington's judgement about what is practical and desirable on the strategic plane. They also will be less inhibited over demanding a say on purposes and outcomes. The net effect is that the United States will feel pressured to yield a larger measure of its autonomy on strategic nuclear decisions. One remarkable feature of this emerging situation is that the Alliance will be testing its skill at genuinely collective decision-making under fluid diplomatic conditions that demand adept handling and orchestration.

5. The Out-of-Area Problem. The handling of out-of-area questions may well be the most drastically affected by any reworking of Alliance arrangements, and by the evolution of new burden-sharing patterns. The structure of the Alliance always has been marked by a striking asymmetry: the disparity between the global span of the United States' political interests and military commitments, on the one hand, and the geographically restricted security focus of its principal allies on the other. The reasons for it are well known. The profound fatigue of two world wars was heightened by the wrenching process of decolonisation whose net effect was to narrow further the Europeans' range of active diplomacy.

The resulting division of labour (which, of course, was also a sharing of labour) was tolerable for all parties so long as certain conditions were met: the availability of ample resources to fund America's global effort; a vague but real consensus on the desirability of the United States playing the role of both 'world policeman' and law-giver; *and* general satisfaction with the way America did the job.

There was always an anomalous and ironic aspect to this arrangement. The broad context of America's security responsibilities was widely taken as evidence of its almost limitless capabilities rather than as reason for lightening the load it bore in Europe. I am reminded of the querulous taxpayer who complained 'taxes are the penalty I pay for not being unemployed.' To draw a rough analogy, it can be said that a disproportionate share of NATO's defence burden is the reward given the United States for its brave performance in carrying it elsewhere. Admittedly, the facts in support of this last declaration are in dispute. But I do believe it fair to say that a tacit approval of those wide-ranging American responsibilities often has not been reciprocated by a forthcoming attitude by Alliance partners on the distribution of costs for the maintenance of European security arrangements.

These asymmetries are now being highlighted (tendentiously by some) as the age of American 'hegemony' fades. Economic constraints on the United States, accompanied by frictions with financial and trading partners, are calling into question its ability and will to perform its accustomed work-horse role. The process of adjustment that will lead the Europeans to take a greater hand in their defence implies both more independence and wider responsibilities. It cannot fail to lead to greater assertiveness on those matters that fall outside NATO's purview but which touch important European interests (the Persian Gulf being the outstanding case in point).

Similarly, it is hard to imagine an America—heavily in debt to its allies and following a regimen of austerity—taking the initiative to protect a collective stake in an area where European (and Japanese) economic interests are so disproportionate to American ones. That convenient division of labour which until now presumed the United States would be out front shoring up political order in the great reaches of the world outside Europe, no longer appears viable. With privileges go burdens. Enhanced European prerogatives on matters of collective interest imply greater responsibility. So too does a more equally balanced co-operative effort to ensure international economic well-being imply venturing into those domains where economics and politics meet. The inevitable outcome will be an incremental globalisation of European foreign policy.

Outcomes

The picture of NATO's future that I have painted up to this point has stressed change. It also has highlighted the difficulties that the Alliance will face in accommodating itself to a diminished American role as its leader—a logical consequence of America's structural economic problems. This prospect though is not offered as a firm prediction of things to come; nor is it complete. Continuity will be at least as important a part of the future as change. Little is predetermined; actual alterations in Alliance relationships will be a matter of degree; and ultimate outcomes will depend on the sagacity and will of NATO states.

Too much of the discussion about America's so-called 'decline' has the flavour of economic determinism to it—if not predestination. There is no basis in our experience or in current realities that obliges us to accept passively a fate so confidently etched. It is public policy and political institutions that will determine how the future unfolds (operating, we must acknowledge, within parameters set by economics as well as by politics). It is there that we should look for clues as to how we might better master the currents of change and gain purchase on evolving international relations. Getting to a satisfactory new equilibrium depends on three factors:

First—for the United States, how much of its leadership disposition and will to an international activism it retains while going through an inescapable process of reappraisal and reassessment;

Second—for the European members of the Alliance, individually and collectively, how ready they are to deal with an America which truly has been reduced to *primus inter pares*—and in some economic spheres no longer even *primus*;

Third—for all parties, the shape they give to new and modified institutions for consultation and collaboration in support of this last declaration are in dispute.*

In any look at the future, the first and foremost question asked concerns the credibility of the United States' commitment to European security and its reliability as an ally. On this central point, one need not hesitate to say that that commitment is irrevocable. America is not about to withdraw from Europe, folding its tents and stealing off into the night. There is no politically significant body of opinion that advocates such action. The debate is over what size and type of physical military presence is called for, and economically supportable, to meet that commitment. The proposition that fundamental American interests are tied to the security and prosperity of Western Europe is accepted by all shades of policy relevant thinking.

Nothing basic has changed either with regard to the pledge to use nuclear force, if necessary, to protect the European members of the Alliance. Understandably, any suggestion of revision in NATO formats, plans or forces raises uneasy feelings about the credibility of an American undertaking that puts the population of the United States at grave risk for the sake of its allies. Anxiety is intrinsic to a situation where the Europeans depend on the United States for their ultimate deterrent. Some small neurosis on this score is not unhealthy in an alliance that bridges oceans and lives in the presence of an enormously powerful enemy. At the same time, we should recognise that nothing degrades deterrent credibility like worrying about it out loud. Were there ever anything that might induce the Soviets to take seriously a possible failure of American will, or, even more pertinent, serious European doubts about American will, it would be an endless bout of hand-wringing and breast-beating over whether 'the Americans really mean it, and what if they don't.' For it is a classic truth that it takes more to reassure an ally than to deter an enemy—since the latter knows its own intention and what it risks while the former knows neither its enemy nor its ally with complete assurance.

While one can affirm these judgements with reasonable confidence on the most critical issue for the Alliance, some grounds for concern remain about the American aptitude for its vocation as a great world power; or, to put the question somewhat differently, its appetite for that role when bedevilled by chronic economic difficulties and no longer enjoying the luxury of redundant power resources. Our earlier discussion about American morale stressed the element of self-doubt that is appearing in the

---

*External factors constitute of course a fourth variable. The largest being the direction of events in the Soviet Union. Much that the NATO allies do or don't do will have a bearing on developments to the East, although a caution is in order as to the limits of the West's ability to affect what happens to the East.

American collective psyche. Its causes are multiple, the loss of economic primacy being only one of them. The economic situation should be seen as contributory to a more generalised awareness of American vulnerability. It is manifestly vulnerable to foreign competitors in trade and finance; it is vulnerable to the wilfulness of other states and peoples who have proven resistant to American appeals and American power; and it is vulnerable to its own mythology that there are certainties to the world and that the United States has a special calling to realise them.

Stated in abstract, these notions might well seem too nebulous to serve as guides to American behaviour. Moreover, one could find abundant evidence that Washington is conducting its foreign affairs with a deliberate realism that belies any suggestion of spiritual malaise. So there is; and that evidence partially reassures us about the stability of American foreign policy. However, it would be to our collective misfortune to ignore the signs of distress that do exist.

Whatever weight we attach to this diagnosis, this is a juncture in the history of Atlantic relations when the United States could benefit from some reassurance (and so benefit the Alliance as a whole). One form of reassurance is to reiterate the point that America's troubled economic state reflects, in part, the fact that it is a victim of its own success. After all, it was the avowed goal of American national policy to bolster the economic strength of its friends in Western Europe and Japan. It laboured mightily towards this end and achieved a result of which it should be justifiably proud. What we are seeing now is, in part at least, the culmination of a process of normalisation. The predominant position in all spheres held by the United States in the first decades after the Second World War was an historical anomaly, which American policy implicitly recognised as such. So, as one commentator has remarked, '(it) is scarcely logical to feel nostalgic about an era that we sought so hard to bring to a close.'[7]

Another, more tangible, form of reassurance would be for the European members of NATO to affirm, with as little equivocation as domestic circumstances permit, that they can do more to defend themselves. Self-respect, as much as Alliance viability, dictates as much. It should be viewed as part of a collective Alliance commitment to face new realities unblushingly. More burden sharing by Western Europe is the counterpart to a sober American facing-up to the necessity of putting its financial house in order. Failure to do so, on the part of each, increases the odds on a self-fulfilling retrenchment by America and the perpetuation of ambivalence in Europe about how much independence from America it wants and can tolerate.

The European Side

An element of ambivalence has always existed in the European Allies' attitude toward the predominant American role in the Alliance. Varying by country and in time, it never has been entirely absent. Now it is being magnified by shifts in the external strategic environment as well as by re-examination of burdens and responsibilities within the Alliance. In the past, it surfaced repeatedly in the recurrent bouts of anxiety about the American readiness to sacrifice its cities for the defence of Europe. These sporadic outbreaks of nervousness were interspersed by less frequent eruptions of concern lest rash American actions entangle the Allies in a conflict not of their choosing. General de Gaulle was especially keen on raising this latter spectre. It has experienced a considerable revival during the Reagan years as many were upset by his confrontational stance in the Middle East and his implacable hostility toward the Soviet Union. Progress on arms control, and the general easing of East/West tensions, have moderated fears in the latter regard (while leaving a strong residue of sentiment in some circles that the United States is as great a contributor to inter-bloc tensions as is the Soviet Union).

The visceral feeling that Western Europe 'can't live with the United States but can't live without her' has only exceptionally affected major policy decisions. As an expression of a situationally defined dilemma, though, it may have a bearing on how smoothly NATO is able to make accommodations to a partial role adjustment among its members. Unless the Atlantic partners resolve on the terms of a more equitable partnership, one can foresee endless friction both between Europe and America *and* among Europeans over who should do what—with what expectation of privileges and burdens. Resentment over American reluctance to relinquish some of its prerogatives (strategically, in defining arms control objectives with the Soviets and operationally, on matters of command, weapons of deployment, and force disposition) could be aggravated by a feeling that the United States has left Europe in the lurch by, for example, unilaterally scaling back the number of ground troops in Europe or committing itself to negotiate the reduction of some classes of arms (aircraft) deemed particu-larly important by European members of the Alliance. On their side, European governments would face the challenge of a concerted defence effort without either the full facilitating presence of American leadership *or* the catalyst that a more precipitate devolution of defence responsibilities might provide (not to mention the weakening of the manifest Soviet threat as a unifying force).

It is unrealistic, no doubt, to expect a well-defined and unified response to any American retrenchment that might be forthcoming. Each European member of NATO has its own perception of what reality is (in Europe and beyond), and its own preferred vision of what security arrangements should look like. In addition, each has a domestic constituency with its peculiar features. But one senses that the goal of attaining greater freedom of manoeuvre is gaining popularity. Greater independence has been urged upon Europe through the shock therapy of American unilateralism: in

Reykjavik, on Iran, and—not least—in conducting its financial affairs as if its economic partners/allies were idle bystanders. Furthermore, objective economic and political realities suggest the logic of exercising greater independence. As Lawrence Freedman has put it, the aim should not be

> a grand new West European entity to take over American responsibilities but a growing prominence for European states in collectively managing security problems.[8]

How one 'gets there from here' is the $64 question. Some of the necessary conditions for success are identifiable. There is first the 'negative'—to be avoided. Unilateralism is the great saboteur of constructive Alliance diplomacy. Generally speaking, behaviour has been improving on this count.[9] Washington, for its part, has taken pains to involve its European partners in the preparation and conduct of strategic arms controls negotiations to a greater extent than in the past. Regrettably, the egregious lapse at Reykjavik opened old wounds which are only partly healed by the tactful handling of the INF negotiations. The lesson must be more fully learned that leadership in the future is not a matter of unilateral example; instead, it expresses itself in the active concerting of positions with other governments.[10]

Stated more positively, co-operation needs to be grounded on the principle of diplomatic equality (even if power and responsibilities remain unevenly distributed across policy spheres). Consultation is one key feature of a more 'egalitarian' approach. Access to internal decision-making is another. The latter will be of particular importance during a period of transition in which Washington's relations with allies/economic partners move gradually away from reliance on American tutelary leadership. In the past, Washington often acted as if it were natural for other governments to wait quietly while it went through the elaborate and opaque process of fashioning a policy. The product then was presented as revealed truth made all the more sacrosanct by the impenetrable method of its formulation. Fruitful collaboration in the future will entail opening the American decision-making process to the views of other governments at earlier stages. That will be no small accomplishment.

There can be no serious burden sharing without power sharing, above all the power over collective decisions.

For their part, the Europeans need to be more forthright and open in acknowledging the parochialism that frequently colours their approach on economic and security issues alike. The full implications of power sharing on that side of the Atlantic is that the subordination of narrow national interest for the collective good must be done voluntarily, and not portrayed habitually as grudging response to the importuning of an Alliance leader (who too easily is depicted in public as exploiting its power while in private is acknowledged to be exercising its proper authority, e.g. the Pershing deployment). These old habits of mind and behaviour will not disappear overnight. But there are features of the Alliance that will facilitate making the transition relatively smooth: there is still a common strategic frame of reference; there is a well-developed institutional memory; and there is easy communication.

Rough-spots there certainly will be. To negotiate the course without serious mishap is the task of diplomacy. The diplomatic calling, after all, is to compose differences and to fashion means to achieve common purposes. For the United States this means a new and different kind of responsibility. America must reinvent statecraft. The world that is transforming itself before our eyes will be placing exceptional demands on the professional skill and adroitness of American foreign policy. As financial and trade considerations are integrated with security and political concerns, the scope of foreign policy will be widened; so will the extent of consultation with partners. Finesse and artful orchestration may not have been hallmarks of American diplomacy in the past; they will be the preconditions for meeting American national interests in the future.

Notes

1. I am indebted to Professor Benjamin M Friedman of Harvard University for illuminating the interplay between the two deficits and their long-term consequences. See his penetrating diagnosis of the United States' economic predicament, *Day of Reckoning: The Consequences of American Economic Policy Under Reagan and After.* New York: Random House, 1988.
2. Paul Kennedy *The Rise and Fall of the Great Powers.* New York: Random House, 1987. Kennedy's scholarship is impeccable and his mastery of historical data impressive. Yet one is drawn up short by declarations such as: 'the most worrying situation of all [Mexico] is just to the south of the United States, and makes the Polish 'crisis' for the USSR seem small by comparison.' p. 517. It is hard to know what to make of a man whose erudition walks hand in hand with such profound ignorance.
3. America's leadership role, even in attenuated form, is being opened to critical scrutiny as never before. Especially visible has been the appearance of intellectual iconoclasts who dispute the necessity or virtue of continued international activism. They are the 'decline of America' school. This body of opinion calls for a reworking of Alliance relations and lobbies for a major scaling back of American commitments. While still a minority within the foreign policy establishment (and among the informed public), it is vocal, active and enjoys considerable sympathy among Congressmen and their staffs. Their common theme has become a recognisable feature of the American political landscape. Its leitmotif is that the American financial crisis rooted in the overextension of American political commitments, defence obligations and military resources. The twin deficits are seen as a direct consequence of allowing commitments to outstrip means. America's long-standing geopolitical position, it is argued, is simply incompatible with a durable financial and monetary balance. Devolution of a good share of the United States' defence burdens on to its allies is the essential element in a strategy of retrenchment, which in turn is the precondition to restoring American solvency and preserving its influence on the world scene.

    In this critical frame of reference, NATO figures prominently (as does Japan, obviously). The litany professes four articles of belief that comprise this world view.

    (i) Europe is less important than it used to be—because the locus of world economic power is shifting to East Asia and because a Soviet Union absorbed with its own internal problems poses a diminished threat.

(ii) Europe has refused to pay its fair share of the burden for defending itself.
(iii) Europe is therefore the logical place for the United States to find the lion's share of necessary reductions in defence spending.
(iv) Scaling down American forces in Europe makes strategic sense given the reduction in the Soviet Union's capability of launching aggressive warfare and the effectiveness of the 'existential deterrence' produced by American nuclear forces in and around Europe.

The pieces of this overview fit together in a logically coherent and reassuring (in some respects) strategy. The source of the United States' economic predicament has been identified, it can be dealt with, and in ways that in no way diminish American security while relieving it of some vexatious and unnecessary obligations. Its attractiveness in the current resource-scarce, inward-looking and vaguely anxious American political climate is clearly visible. However dubious its assumptions and facile its recommendations, it does constitute one of the frames of reference that will be competing for primacy as the United States passes through a period of reappraisal and adjustment.

The near 'ideal' statement of this viewpoint has been offered by David P Callio, Harold van B Cleveland, and Leonard Silk in 'The Dollar and the Defense of the West', *Foreign Affairs*, Spring 1988, Vol. 66, No. 4. See also the revealing 'A New Grand Strategy', by James Chase in *Foreign Policy*, No. 70, Spring 1988.

4. W W Rostow *Foreign Affairs*, Summer 1988, Vol. 66, No. 5.
5. Report of the Commission on Integrated Long-Term Strategy, *Discriminate Deterrence*. Washington: GPO, January 1988.
6. Samuel P Huntington 'Coping With The Lippmann Gap', *Foreign Affairs: America and the World 1987/88*, Summer 1988, Vol. 63, No. 5.
7. James Schlesinger 'The Eagle and the Bear', *Foreign Affairs*, Summer 1988, Vol. 63, No. 5.
8. Lawrence Freedman 'Managing Alliances', *IISS Annual Meeting*, September 1988.
9   For a scathing critique of American conduct see Michael Howard's 'A European Perspective on the Reagan Years', *Foreign Affairs*. America and the World 1987/88.
10. This point is developed by Joseph S Nye, Jr. in 'Understanding U.S. Strength', *Foreign Policy*, No. 72, Fall 1988.

PART 4

Dialogue of the Deaf?

CHAPTER 7

American Perceptions of NATO and the European Community

MARTIN J HILLENBRAND

Current American perceptions of NATO and the European Community can obviously not be detached from the post-war history of those organisations and the United States' relationship with them, but it is also true that the period ahead will present a number of new problems that may well worsen such perceptions. From the outset the United States lacked any clear, coherent and universally accepted conceptual framework for its relationship with Europe. Indeed, the early thrust of American policy at the end of the war was to occupy a defeated Germany for a short period, and to turn over the longer-term problem of the country to the Soviets, the French and the British who would know better how to deal with those difficult Teutons. The pell-mell demobilisation of our victorious armies was symptomatic of this attitude. The collapse of the wartime alliance and the advent of the Cold War changed all that. It quickly became clear that we were indefinitely stuck in Europe, but even after the creation of NATO in 1949, a significant number of Americans continued to maintain that this whole situation was abnormal, and that sooner or later—preferably sooner—we should be able to bring our troops back to the United States. President Eisenhower himself believed this, while loyally supporting the Alliance that he had previously led as Supreme Allied Commander Europe.

Once NATO had come into existence, some other Americans, including an influential State Department official like Livingston Merchant, saw in the early thrust towards European unity, represented by the Coal and Steel Community and the Treaty to Create a European Defence Community (the EDC), a threat to the ultimate viability of the Alliance of which we were now an integral part. This was a line of thinking that was to emerge in various guises during subsequent years, particularly as American quarrels with the Community grew more intense.

On the other hand, the main thrust of American policy during the 1950s was strongly to support the idea of European unity and the incipient

103

organisations that seemed to embody it. A number of idealistic young State and Treasury Department officials assigned to the special mission in Paris headed by Ambassador David Bruce, became dedicated Europeanists. Although the mission was also accredited as the United States' representation to the Coal and Steel Community in Luxembourg, it quickly emerged that its primary function was to do everything it could to get the French National Assembly to ratify the EDC Treaty. It obviously could not bring direct pressure on a parliamentary body, but by pressing successive French governments to take action, and by meeting various French requests for so-called *conditions préalables*, members of the Bruce Mission hoped that the Assembly would finally pass the necessary ratifying legislation. The whole effort collapsed in the summer of 1954 after Pierre Mendès France became Prime Minister. The cause had a been a noble one, and like most historical failures it left psychological scars. Some have argued that the European movement never really recovered the idealistic élan that had gone into the support of the European Defense Community concept.

Be that as it may, the next effort to move towards European unity came with the creation of the European Economic Community by the 1957 Treaty of Rome. This time ratification followed, and the Treaty came into effect. Once again the United States supported a European initiative towards unity. The formula that later became almost a Washington truism was that the United States would be prepared to accept the disadvantages to us that European economic unity might bring because of the greater advantages to be gained from European political union. This was to prove to be a hard doctrine to accept in practice, but for many years it remained the basis for American policy towards a Community that, from the viewpoint of Washington, became ever more a source of economic problems. Dispute after dispute arose in the trade area, particularly as a result of the Common Agricultural Policy, but in the final analysis the State Department was generally able to influence the reaching of compromise solutions that avoided an outright break.

Meanwhile, all was not peace and harmony within NATO, but the Alliance continued to achieve its essential purpose of deterring Soviet aggression. The 1952 Lisbon force goals never had a realistic chance of being attained, and the increasing reliance during the 1950s and 1960s on tactical nuclear weapons deployed in Europe, and the extended deterrence provided by American strategic forces, led to internal political disputes within NATO countries, particularly the Federal Republic of Germany, over the appropriate arming of the Alliance. The Soviets provided the great unifier by precipitating a five-year-long Berlin crisis during which the debate over tactics and deployments became secondary to the need for unity against what seemed like a fundamental challenge to the Western political position in Central Europe.

During the Kennedy Administration, the President and some of his advisers tried to find a conceptual framework, or at least a figure of speech, for the European–American relationship. The unlikely metaphor of a dumbbell came into usage, with Europe and the United States at each end of the connecting central rod. One also spoke of two pillars, Europe and the United States, presumably sustaining the Alliance. Kennedy said he had 'a Grand Design' for the free world. But all this was mere rhetoric. It did not contribute anything really new, either conceptually or operationally, to a relationship that had always presumed a mutuality of interest in preventing Soviet domination of Western Europe and in achieving steady economic growth. The great theory continued to be lacking, and perhaps there was none to be found for what was essentially a derivative of cultural and ethnic heritage as well as of military and geographic reality.[1]

American Attitudes Towards NATO During the Middle Post-War Period

Once the Berlin crisis had subsided, a new set of problems, essentially economic in nature, began to affect American attitudes towards the Alliance. One military holdover, however, continued to plague the European–American relationship. In 1960 the Eisenhower Administration had proposed the creation of a so-called Multilateral Force (MLF) to meet what it felt to be a European psychological requirement to have at least one finger on a portion of the nuclear deterrent in the Alliance. The idea was to have some 500 Polaris missiles deployed on the decks of surface vessels (probably old Second World War Victory ships taken out of moth-balls). While the ultimate control of warheads would remain in American hands under some form of double-key system, this clumsily elaborate, and perhaps unworkable system, was to provide an offset to the more than 500 Soviet S-4 and S-5 intermediate range missiles targeted on Western Europe which, despite their lack of accuracy, had enough destructive power to blow the continental members of the Alliance, and Britain as well, off the face of the globe.

The Kennedy Administration adopted the MLF as its own. The Europeans, on the other hand, were never enchanted by the proposal, but what was originally intended as something to meet a presumed European psychological requirement gradually became an American cause and, in our view, a test of European fidelity to the Alliance. Washington sent out teams of advocates to visit European capitals and to sell governments on the virtues of the MLF. Without great enthusiasm, a few governments agreed to accept the idea, and the German Foreign Minister Gerhart Schroeder publicly argued in its favour.

When he took over as President, Lyndon Johnson began to have doubts in the face of reports from Europe that the United States was pushing something that few if any NATO members really wanted. Finally he killed the whole proposal, sawing off in the process the limb on which Foreign Minister Schroeder had been sitting. Needless to say, those years of attempted American salesmanship to reluctant European governments did little to enhance mutual respect within NATO, but they did provide the kind of setting within which Secretary of Defense McNamara's idea of a Nuclear Planning Group (NPG) was destined to be an organisational success.

By the late 1950s, it had become apparent that the period of United States balance of payments dominance over Western Europe had come to an end. One logical consequence was that, for the first time in the post-war period, some Americans began to question the continuing large-scale American military presence in Europe, not on strategic grounds, but on its affordability. While it was politically impossible to ask for a restoration of occupation costs as such, smacking of the military government era, the euphemism 'offset agreements' provided an acceptable formula for various forms of West German financial assistance that survived until 1975. The negotiations for the renewal of these agreements made small contribution to German–American friendship although, after a protracted periodic diplomatic tug-of-war, usually requiring high-level intervention before the end, the two countries would emerge with a bundle of compromises that left no one completely happy. The expression 'burden sharing' crept into usage, while Senator Mansfield began his annual, if unsuccessful, effort to legislate sizeable unilateral cuts of United States forces in Europe.

What this all added up to was an interlocking series of problems that negatively affected American perceptions of the Alliance, but never exploded into the kind of self-destructive frenzy that could have done permanent damage to the basic purposes of NATO.

Changing American Attitudes Towards the European Economic Community

American theoretical support of the European Economic Community as the principal expression of European unification continued into the 1970s, but the growing conflict of economic interests between the Community and the United States proved to be a constant source of strain. Symptomatic of a changing mood in Washington was the deliberate omission in the 1971 Report of the President to the Congress of any reference to the hallowed formula, still to be found in President Nixon's 1970 Report, to the effect that

'the possible economic price of a truly unified Europe is outweighed by the gain in the political vitality of the West as a whole.'[2]

Although there were other areas of dispute, the main culprit from the

American point of view was the Community's Common Agricultural Policy (CAP), which appeared to be rapidly turning Europe into a heavily subsidised area of surplus agricultural production, and away from a group of countries normally importing a considerable quantity of American agricultural products. Given the concomitant problem of American farm surpluses, the mood in the Congress, particularly among representatives from the states most involved, as well as the Department of Agriculture, turned bitter. Although the world-wide agricultural shortages of the middle 1970s provided a period of relief, the conflict was bound to emerge again, particularly as the green revolution in some developing countries, and the competition of large grain-producers such as Canada, Australia and the Argentine added to the surplus-disposal problem.

Even those American officials who had experienced the excitement of the formative 1950s found themselves hard pressed to defend European practices that clearly seemed destined to damage US economic interests without any compensatory real movement towards European political union. Apart from the CAP, the Gaullist model of a *Europe des patries* seemed to be the ascendent model, and the enlargement of the Community (though the United States had strongly favoured British entry, partly perhaps because de Gaulle had so fervently opposed it) threatened only to make political unity an even more distant goal.

Once the United States had emerged from the trauma of Watergate, the full implications of the breakdown of the Bretton Woods system began to become clear. Not only was gold dethroned as the standard of value, but the floating exchange rate system, sanctified at Jamaica in 1975, foreshadowed a new era of uncertainty in international economic relations. The dollar was still mighty as a world currency, but the domestic economy that ultimately sustained it had begun to show those signs of weaknesses that, during the 1980s, only a perverse and exorbitant form of Keynesianism could camouflage, even in part. Many thinking Americans became progressively more uneasy about the crumbling international competitiveness of the American economy, but the European Economic Community—in 1983 to become simply the European Community—had at least ceased to be the sole global transgressor, although still the *bête noire* of American agriculture. The two oil shocks of 1973 and 1978–79 actually brought Europeans and Americans somewhat closer together in facing the common problems of oil-importing countries. Another binding factor was the advent of economic summitry, as meagre as the concrete achievements of these annual assemblages of the great generally turned out to be.

One can, of course, tend to overemphasise the role of problems in an account of this kind. Given the ethnic origins of most Americans, and the cultural ties that many still have with Europe, the natural disposition has generally tended to be favourable towards things European. The Holocaust and other Nazi atrocities have cast their shadow over whole generations, but the steady stream of American tourists to Europe over the post-war years has been a visible symptom of the ties that continue to bind. Relatively few Americans really know very much, if anything, about the European Community of yesterday or today. The perceptions that matter are those of the educated élites, and even here the gaps in knowledge can be surprising. There is a somewhat greater constituency with at least some rudimentary perceptions of NATO, given the number of military personnel who have served as officers or enlisted men under various NATO commands, as well as the somewhat broader community of government officials and academics involved in the handling or study of related military and strategic subjects.

More Recent NATO Developments Affecting American Perceptions

The media have generally tended to overstate the intensity of the various crises that have afflicted NATO over the years of its existence. Reviewing the reporting of the past, one might come away with the impression that the Alliance has been in a constant state of turmoil and dissension—a gloomy picture far from the reality. Nevertheless, the admitted periods of crisis have in nearly all cases involved the relationship of the United States to one or more of its allies. While the expulsion of NATO civilian and military headquarters and forces from France in 1966–67 was, in essence, a form of retribution by President de Gaulle against what he regarded as Anglo-Saxon domination of the Alliance, as well as British and American rejection of the triumvirate that he desired, a chief practical result was to necessitate new lines of supply for American forces in Germany running parallel to the putative Central Front—an untenable situation from a military point of view for those who thought in terms of conventional warfare in Europe. American commanders were naturally unhappy about this development, but swallowed it as a bitter yet unavoidable political reality.

Although largely confined to academic circles in the United States, the advent, during the late 1950s and 1960s, of a revisionist school of diplomatic historians raised troubling questions about a fundamental premise of the rationale for NATO: that the Soviet Union bore the primary responsibility for the Cold War. Academic fashions move in seemingly inevitable cycles, and in a few years the post-revisionists appeared on the scene with a more balanced version of events. It would be foolish to deny, however, that many young diplomatic historians and teachers of international relations came under the influence of revisionist mentors to a greater or lesser extent.[3] In a later era, a more sophisticated variant of revisionism emerged in the argument that, whatever the convictions of the NATO founding fathers, the Soviet Union never intended to launch an offensive against Western Europe, and that consequently the entire military structure of the

Alliance was built on a false premise.[4] Once again, the policy élites were only marginally affected by such heretical thinking, but the implications for perceptions of NATO were obvious if it were to become widely accepted doctrine.

Attempts to legislate unilateral American troop reductions in Europe subsided somewhat during the Nixon years as the United States and a group of its NATO allies entered into what were to prove interminable Mutual and Balanced Force Reductions (MBFR) negotiations in Vienna. The argument proved effective that it made little sense to give away a negotiating counter in advance by making prior unilateral American troop withdrawals without getting anything in exchange for them. It would be less than frank to deny that this was among the motives that led a group of State Department officials strongly to support the initiation of MBFR negotiations.

STRATEGIC AND ARMS CONTROL ISSUES

Issues of strategy, arms control and weapons deployment came to the fore in NATO during the late 1970s and early 1980s. Although the discussion of strategy never entirely ceased within the Alliance, there had been a comparative lull for a decade, once US Secretary of Defense McNamara succeeded in 1967 in obtaining acceptance of flexible response as basic NATO strategy—a strategy that made no one completely happy, but seemed best ordinated to the weapons deployments and individual national dispositions of member officials and military leaders. However, the data with respect to delivery systems and warheads accepted by both sides, and embodied in the SALT I and SALT II negotiations, had effectively disposed of any lingering remnants of massive retaliation as a basis for American extended deterrence. At the same time more sophisticated observers had concluded that it was not certainty about the use of strategic missiles that constituted the essence of nuclear deterrence, but rather the uncertainty about the possibility of their use in an escalating military crisis.

Nevertheless, the whole conceptual structure seemed to be eroding at the base as such commentators as Henry Kissinger publicly questioned it: in a speech that he made in 1979 at a Brussels conference sponsored by the Georgetown Center for Strategic and International Studies and the Paris-based Atlantic Institute for International Affairs. Whether with perverse intent or due to a sudden overdose of honesty, he in effect told the Europeans that they were foolish to count on an American President's risking the destruction of his country by using strategic nuclear weapons in the defence of Europe. The reaction in Europe was bound to be sensational. In fact, Kissinger himself realised this, after conferring with his colleagues, and hastily called a corrective press conference. But the damage was done. The press had carefully noted what he had said in his speech, and reported accordingly.[5] NATO and State Department officials tried to throw verbal water on the fire, but Kissinger's sensational statement stuck in the European mind.

The years that followed also proved to be the period when anxious right-wing American strategists spoke of a window of vulnerability. The argument here started with the premise that, because of the vulnerability of American land-based Minuteman missiles, the Soviets might be tempted to make a pre-emptive strike with a sufficient portion of their superior land-based missile force (particularly their 308 SS-18s with ten 'mirved' warheads on each) to wipe out all our Minutemen. Then an American President would be faced with the decision of whether to retaliate with our sea-based nuclear missiles, which did not have a real counterforce capability, and thus expose American centres of population to annihilation by the more accurate unused Soviet land-based missile. Arguments of this kind played an important role not only in creating uneasiness with the general strategic situation, but also in providing a potent argument against ratification of the SALT II Treaty by such groups as the Committee for the Present Danger. While this essentially American debate made its own distinctive contribution to European uneasiness, particularly when it became clear that ratification of the SALT II Treaty, favoured by most Europeans, would not take place, it also engendered a peculiar kind of American resentment against those NATO allies who seemed incapable of understanding the distinctive American concerns with the overall strategic situation.

While this was going on, another development took place that raised considerable doubts in the United States about the steadfastness of European members of the Alliance. During the mid-1970s the Soviet Union began a major deployment of SS-20 medium range missiles to replace its obsolete SS-4 and SS-5 medium range missiles. These new missiles were mobile, 'mirved' with three warheads each, and highly accurate. In effect, they seemed to place all significant military targets in Western Europe in jeopardy, as well as any other objectives that might be targeted. The initial American response was to reassure the Europeans that all important targets in the Soviet Union and Eastern Europe were covered by American strategic forces or our sea-launched missile capabilities.[6] While this might have seemed like an adequate response in the abstract, given the doubts that had been raised about the reliability of the United States strategic deterrent, it did not go far enough to meet European psychological requirements. Chancellor Helmut Schmidt raised the whole issue in the Alistair Buchan Memorial Lecture that he delivered in London in 1977 and this set in motion a chain of causation that led to the American offer to deploy 108 Pershing II and 464 cruise missiles in Western Europe. As had happened before, most notably in the case of MLF, what started out as an American attempt to comply with assumed European desires gradually turned into an

American cause, and European willingness to accept the weapons deployments involved became a test of loyalty to the Alliance.

The massive demonstrations against deployment of the new weapons, particularly in West Germany, but also in Great Britain, the Netherlands, Denmark, Belgium and even Italy, which followed the NATO Ministerial Council decision of December, 1979, to proceed with total or partial deployment if negotiations with the Soviets did not commensurately reduce the number of SS-20s, could not help but raise additional doubts in the United States about the fidelity of European populations to the purposes of NATO. Heavy media coverage brought home both the intensity of these demonstrations, and the strong anti-American strain as well as more general anti-nuclear sentiment underlying them.

As in other instances of this kind, I am talking about essentially élite opinion in the United States. The average American, educated in fields other than international relations, scarcely gives a stray thought to NATO, although an occasional editorial, column or cartoon may arouse hostile reactions towards the 'ungrateful Europeans'.

When the Reagan Administration took over in January, 1981, it brought into office a mixture of sentiments. Apart from the general mood of enhanced hostility towards the Soviet Union, it included some officials such as Secretary of State Alexander Haig and ACDA Director Eugene Rostow, with strong dedication to the classical purposes of the Alliance, but it also included others who were either essentially Pacific-oriented or bore strong resentment against Europeans for allegedly not pulling their weight in the Alliance. The strong anti-Soviet bias of the President during the early Reagan years effectively prevented the latter group from having much influence on traditional policy.

ISSUES OF TRADE AND TECHNOLOGY TRANSFER

Another aspect of differing American and European evaluations and policies, while, of course, partially economic in context, came to a head in the early Reagan years over trade and technology transfer to the Soviet Union and its Eastern European allies. American views on this subject, as expressed in the Paris Coordinating Committee (COCOM) and through other channels, had traditionally been more stringent than those of other NATO countries, but the Reagan Administration—dominated in this policy area by the Defense Department—favoured even more severe restrictions. One had the impression that, grain excepted, almost any commodity trade with the Soviet Union was bad since, directly or indirectly, it could be argued, it permitted some diversion of scarce resources to the military part of the economy. The issue came to a head in 1981–82 as the Reagan Administration tried to apply sanctions to American multinational firms operating in Europe, and even to European firms that had ties with

American firms, in order to halt the Soviet acquisition of pipeline equipment and related compressors intended for delivery of natural gas from the Soviet Union to Western Europe. The whole imbroglio turned out to be fiasco for the United States; claims of extraterritorial extension of United States laws and regulations had long been a source of irritation to European, or for that matter Canadian, allies. His attempt to modify United States policy was among the factors that cost Alexander Haig his position as Secretary of State. His successor, George Shultz, skilfully managed to kick the pipeline issue under the rug.[7] The general conflict over trade policy with the Communists, however, continued, and it is fair to say that the perceptions of hardliners in Washington of European attitudes on this issue could only be strongly negative. As the Reagan administration in its later years moved towards a more politically conciliatory position with respect to the Soviet Union, some of the heat naturally went out of this form of the trade issue. The divisions over policy among officials in Washington remained, with the Pentagon continuing to exercise a strong influence. The implications one way or the other for a weakened American international economy had not yet really been factored into current judgements on the issue.

ARMS CONTROL AND THE IMPACT OF GORBACHEV

Meanwhile, as the deployment in Europe of Pershing II and cruise missiles began late in 1982, Americans could not help but note how rapidly the steam had escaped from the mass opposition to such deployment. Such demonstrations as took place seemed relatively miniscule compared to those in the pre-deployment period. Washington had also noted that, despite all their uneasiness, the European governments involved, and especially the German government of Helmut Kohl, had demonstrated the political courage required to accept the new missiles. The NATO position from the outset had been that their deployment would take place only if the Soviet Union showed it was unwilling to negotiate mutual reductions. The initial American position in the International Nuclear Force (INF) talks had been the so-called zero-zero formula, that is, total destruction of the Soviet SS-20s in return for non-deployment of American Pershing II and cruise missiles. Its proponents in the Pentagon thought of it as non-negotiable and therefore a guarantee of failure of the INF talks. Nor could any agreement be reached on partial but equivalent reductions of missiles which had become the Western fallback position. When the deployment of American missiles actually began, the Soviets walked out of the INF talks as well as other ongoing arms control negotiations—a result that ensured continued deployment on both sides and the seeming elimination of any opportunity to halt them or actually reduce the overall totals.

On the whole, this rather complicated prelude to what followed made a positive contribution to American official perceptions of our NATO allies, although questions remained about the shifts in European opinion that had transformed an American attempt to provide new weapons for the defence of Europe into such a divisive issue. What followed, of course, was the coming to power of Mikhail Gorbachev in the Soviet Union, and the changes in Soviet arms control policy that he initiated. On the American side as well, President Reagan adopted a new tack, abandoning much of the rhetoric of invective and evidencing a genuine interest in reaching arms control agreements with the Soviets. The various negotiations in Geneva resumed, and at the Reykjavik summit broad agreements were almost reached, not only on INF but on strategic forces being discussed in the START context, shocking both many Americans and NATO allies, since they came without adequate prior discussion or even consideration in Washington. The fact that only the President's devotion to his Strategic Defense Initiative (SDI) had apparently blocked agreement, could only seem ironic in the light of, at best, only tepid European support for the whole concept. The fact that American expert opinion on the feasibility and desirability of the SDI programme was split down the middle helped to avoid major irritation (outside the Pentagon and segments of the White House) at Europe's reticence fully and unreservedly to endorse SDI.

Gorbachev brought not only a new flexibility to Soviet foreign and security policy; he also greatly improved the quality of Soviet propaganda in Western Europe. Before long reports began to reach Washington, and to appear in the world press, that public opinion in Europe was beginning to shift away from its traditional basic support of American foreign policy, and to credit the Soviet leader with making a greater contribution to peace than President Reagan. A poll taken in the summer of 1988 showed that 71 per cent of West Germans had a 'favourable opinion' of Gorbachev compared with only 41 per cent for Reagan.[8] Another cause of anxiety among some old-line NATO supporters in the US was the fear that the improving relations between the two German states, plus the effect of Gorbachev's propaganda, actually indicated a drifting away from the Alliance by the West Germans as they proceeded down the slippery slope to disengagement and neutralisation. The theorising of French intellectuals and officials on this development also had some impact on the United States, despite the fact that Chancellor Kohl and his political supporters had personally demonstrated their loyalty to the West and its institutions.

For years a favourite subject for discussion at many conferences involving Americans had been the so-called 'successor generation problem'. It was, of course, an entirely legitimate question to ask how a new generation of potential leaders in government and business, who had had no personal experience of the formative post-war period, could be expected to share the evaluations, judgements and support for institutions that derived from that experience. The question was, however, easier to ask than to answer in a satisfactory way. The problem is obviously not only European but also

American, since the perceptions of Europe by younger Americans will derive from an essentially different background of experience from that of their parents.

The growth of East–West summitry, the improvement of Soviet–American relations, and the specific agreements already reached, or in prospect, between the two superpowers might have given rise again to what has been a typically European syndrome. While most Europeans and their governments could only be nervous when superpower relations were bad, and could only wish for their improvement, when that improvement actually took place and led to specific agreements, one kind of nervousness turned into another. The fear has been that the two superpowers would get together behind the backs of the Europeans and negotiate away their interests without full consultation. Americans have been puzzled by this seeming lack of basic confidence in their ally, but it was idle to dismiss it—as was sometimes done—as just another example of how inconsistent the Europeans are capable of being. The Soviet Union's Eastern European allies have sometimes evidenced a similar nervousness. It seemed inherent in the relative power relationship involved. With the rapid process of change underway in the Soviet Union, Poland and Hungary, however, the psychological landscape may well have changed both in the West and the East in this regard.

NATO AND ECONOMICS

While Article 2 of the Treaty establishing the North Atlantic Treaty Organisation, which foresaw NATO as a forum for discussion of economic problems, has always been a dead letter, those problems—particularly those of the United States—are bound to play an increasingly important role as we approach the 1990s. The assumption that, given the will, all things are possible for the American superpower, must inevitably run into the harsh reality that the United States has become by far the world's largest debtor country and will continue to pile up foreign debts as we struggle to reduce our current account and budgetary deficits—both sustainable only as long as foreign lenders continue to invest in the United States. This is not the place to discuss when and how we can restore American competitiveness in international and domestic markets, or make our budgetary deficits more manageable, but it seems axiomatic that American attitudes towards the Alliance as such will inevitably be affected by future European economic behaviour as well as traditional security considerations (both to be discussed later in this essay). This will be particularly the case if President Gorbachev continues to turn inward with his programme of economic reform and adopt a less aggressive military stance.

Future American Perceptions of the European Community

Future American perceptions of the European Community, starting from the relatively low estimate of the present, will obviously largely depend on the behaviour of the Community with respect to those interests the American Government and international businessmen regarded as important. There will be little residual idealism about European unity to temper reactions to Community measures that run counter to those interests. It is difficult to see, for example, how the Common Agricultural Policy—unless it is radically, not merely marginally, overhauled—can be anything but a continuing source of grievance and controversy.

1992 has become the great rallying point for the Community—the year by the end of which, it is agreed, all barriers to trade between the member countries will vanish. Whether the Community can realistically achieve that goal by 1992, or only a few years later, the central question for non-member states, such as the United States, remains whether the basic thrust of EC policy will be in the direction of protectionism or a liberal trading system. Spokesmen for the Community stress that it will be the latter. On the other hand, critics have argued that the whole point of a real common market is to give preferential treatment to its members, and that some form of protectionism against the outside world is inevitable. That may well be the case, and in an era of advancing technology the kinds of preferences extended to agriculture may also apply, in one form or another, to such areas as communications, avionics and aerospace. Experience in the post-Second World War era, however, has shown the frequent unpredictability of economic phenomena.

One can think of several scenarios that, for better or worse, will affect American perceptions of a developing European Community. The most benign would have such a Community turn into a dynamic, outward-looking trading group both with the United States and Asia, while at the same time the United States successfully comes to grips with its external and internal deficits and consequent debt problems which, if not brought under control, threaten seriously to undermine American capacity for leadership and, indeed, for adequate participation in an expanding world economy. There is certainly nothing impossible in all this, provided the quality of leadership and understanding on both sides of the Atlantic is high and uncontrollable negative economic developments do not override rational expectations and the capacity of nations to deal with the problems that confront them.

A more sombre scenario would envisage a continuation of present protectionist trends in the Community and the United States leading to confrontation and 'trade wars'. This could be coupled with a protracted American inability to achieve competitiveness and budgetary control, and hence to halt the rise of its external indebtedness. The dollar would continue to fall and foreign investors become ever more reluctant to sink more money in dollar instruments.

An even more negative scenario would embody the developments in the preceding paragraph, but they would take place within a broader global context of unmanageable debt, overproduction, deflation and depression. Some pessimistic economists see this as likely, and supporters of the Kondratiev long-wave theory think the timing would be about right.

Such scenarios obviously fail to take into account the unpredictable element in economics, or the resourcefulness that our leaders can sometimes demonstrate under pressure. But it would take more optimism than this author can muster to believe that the years ahead will not be troubled ones in the relationship between the United States and the European Community. President Bush will find that the failure of the Reagan Administration to come to grips with the fundamental economic problems that afflict the United States, but to postpone their eruption by foreign-borrowing— and a sort of lopsided internal Keynesianism—will confront him willy nilly with many painful decisions. The European Community will, among others, provide a convenient whipping boy. Writing recently in *The Financial Times*, its knowledgeable correspondent, Anthony Harris, observed that 'American disillusion with Europe in general, and Germany in particular, is becoming an important political fact ... a German-dominated Europe is seen as wedded to stagnation.'[9] Whether or not this is a fair appraisal, it is certainly one shared by many conservative economists who served in the Reagan Administration. It would be a legitimate debating point to remark that their own record fell far short of glorious, but right or wrong never dulled the intensity of emotion that arguments among economists can engender.

It became fashionable during the Reagan years to talk of the 'Pacific Century', implying that Europe would become of secondary interest as we moved towards the year 2000. During his tenure as Special Assistant to the President for Security Affairs, Robert McFarland supported the thesis that the United States needed to shift its priorities away from Europe to the Asian Basin. After all, we now had a larger overall total trade with Asia than with Europe, he argued. He did not mention, of course, that imports constituted most of our trade with Asia, whereas our trade deficit with Europe, while substantial, was essentially a development of the strong dollar years of 1982–85, and their aftermath. The slogan 'Pacific Century', some commentators have pointed out, may in practice not mean what those Americans who mouth it suppose. The assumption of the 'Asia-firsters' has been that the United States will now turn to its relations with Asia and the Europeans will simply have to adjust to this new reality. The counter-argument made by Europeans is that the countries of East Asia measure their economic success in global terms rather than purely as part of a

Pacific system. Moreover, countries like Great Britain and West Germany, since 1986, have had more trade with Eurasia than across the North Atlantic. Furthermore, in the past five years Japan and the newly industrialising countries of East Asia have enlarged their direct foreign investment in the European Community at a rate one-third faster than in the United States.[10] It is far from clear what this all adds up to, but the European Community, as the largest market economy in the world, will be a major competitor of the United States in global markets, and more specifically in Asian markets if and when they progressively open up. Needless to say, as this reality becomes apparent, it will not be without its effect on American perceptions of the Community as a commercial rival.

Although it is difficult to judge precisely how this will all work out, one can predict that the process will also inevitably influence American attitudes with respect to security issues and the future of NATO. This may seem like a truism, but the tendency in the past has been largely to ignore the linkage between American economic and military power. A number of recent books have tried to relate the two, and have generally ended up with rather pessimistic conclusions about the future of the Alliance unless the United States can find new sources of economic and social vitality.[11]

Future American Perceptions of NATO

If its members perceive the underlying threat that brought the North Atlantic Treaty Organisation into existence, and maintained its sense of purpose over the years, as no longer present, NATO would soon cease to serve any useful purpose, although the bureaucracy that has developed in Brussels and elsewhere would fight to the end to preserve jobs and perquisites. Should such a process take place, it will obviously not happen overnight. Recognition of changing realities can come slowly and irregularly. Certainly a majority of Americans interested in such questions continues to perceive NATO as playing an important role in the provision of stability between the superpowers and security in Europe. We are far from the point where that majority, reflected in Washington official opinion as well, would be willing to accept the dissolution of NATO as no longer serving any worthy purpose.

That much having been said, one can also expect further growth of the feeling that the European members are not pulling their full weight in the Alliance, and that American efforts must continue to achieve more equitable sharing of the burden of common defence. On the European side, as former French Foreign Minister Jean François-Poncet has put it,

> The creation of a 'European pillar' is once again a matter of intensive debate
> . . . What is leading the Europeans, and in particular the French and Germans,
> to return to the idea of the 'Europeanisation' of defence in a more precise,

concrete way, is the underlying sense that the United States' defence commitment to Europe will be reduced in the near future and Europeans will have no other choice but to take over military responsibilities, to the extent that is necessary, from their American allies.[12]

Whatever the peculiar French logic contained in this analysis, more and more sophisticated Europeans have come to share a similar viewpoint. Talking about the creation of a European pillar is, of course, much easier than taking the concrete measures to achieve it. Once again, to quote François-Poncet,

> The aim is not to replace the Atlantic defence system with a European one, but rather to shift the balance that now exists within NATO more towards Europe, to reshape the organisation, but to leave the basic Alliance intact.[13]

The point is sometimes made in the United States that we will sooner or later adapt the geographical distribution of our armed forces to the new economic and political structure of the world. Whether or not one regards this type of reasoning as just another version of the 'Pacific Century', I am not persuaded of its logic. If détente between the superpowers reaches a stage that dramatically reduces the need for American forces in Europe, or for that matter for NATO itself, it is difficult to see what the threat elsewhere in the world is likely to be that would necessitate major American military deployments elsewhere. If it does not, the principal area of confrontation will continue to be Central Europe, if one accepts the basic strategic unacceptability of Soviet political control of Western Europe.

Apart from the issue of burden sharing, American supporters of NATO are most likely to be concerned about European trends in public and official opinion that, given further Gorbachev successes in public relations, could move Alliance members, particularly Germany, towards neutralisation. The idea of a European Peace Order (*Europäische Friedensordnung*), with Eastern and Western Europeans again in a harmonious relationship, and with the superpowers retreating to their natural boundaries, has had a certain attraction for German intellectuals and students. The logical result, of course, would be dissolution of the two blocs.

At the same time, Americans not of the conservative right wing have been puzzled by a recent report of a group of leading European research institutions, *The Gorbachev Challenge and European Security*, that warned that the Soviet leader is, in effect, seeking drastic changes in Western defences (read nuclear) before carrying out the basic domestic changes that would reduce the Soviet threat. The study also warned that, as Soviet diplomacy became more dexterous, American foreign policy could complicate Western Europe's ability to defend its interests. The Royal Institute of International

Affairs, the French Institute for International Relations, the Italian International Affairs Institute, the Norwegian Institute of Foreign Affairs and both the German Foreign Policy Association and the Foundation for Science and Politics that sponsored the study, represent a cross-section of traditional European attitudes towards defence and the Alliance.[14] A cynic might argue that this is just another example of the European syndrome that emerges whenever the two superpowers seem to be negotiating seriously, but so far, at least, American élites have not felt it to be a serious hindrance to agreements that might otherwise appear desirable. It is likely, once again, to arouse the petulant reaction that it is impossible to make the Europeans happy, no matter what the United States does.

The years ahead, therefore, promise to be a period of tense confusion in American perceptions of NATO. Commentators like Henry Kissinger will undoubtedly see that the Alliance is in a major crisis as American negotiations with the Soviets promise to eliminate weapons systems upon which the Europeans have come to rely as essential to their security. Others will argue that NATO has weathered many crises in the past, and has always emerged with its basic unity of purpose intact. In the view of this author, economic factors affecting American power and interests are most likely to influence American attitudes towards the Alliance, as well as the European response, plus the development of Soviet policy in the years ahead. It would run counter to experience to think in terms of dramatic changes within a short period of time. Slow evolution in the perceptions of problems and in drawing the logical consequences of those perceptions seems the most likely outcome of the forces operating in the contemporary world.

Notes

1. These opening pages, and much of what follows, are largely based on the personal recollections of the author as an American professional diplomat who was personally involved, to a greater or lesser extent, in the events described.
2. Compare *US Foreign Policy for the 1970s: A New Strategy for Peace, A Report to the Congress by Richard Nixon President of the United States February 18, 1970.* Washington: U.S. Government Printing Office, undated, p. 32, with *U.S. Foreign Policy for the 1970s: Building for Peace, A Report to the Congress by Richard Nixon President of the United States February 25, 1971.* Washington: US Government Printing Office, undated.
3. The best balanced discussion of this whole subject, in the view of the author, is to be found in the various writings of John Lewis Gaddis. See, for example, his *The United States and the Origins of the Cold War 1941–1947.* New York: Columbia University Press, 1972.
4. See, for example, George F. Kennan *The Nuclear Delusion: Soviet–American Relations in the Atomic Age.* New York: Pantheon Books, 1983, p. xii.
5. See, for example, *The New York Times*, September 2, 1974.
6. The author was at the time the American Ambassador in Bonn.
7. For a well-researched account of the natural gas pipeline fiasco, see Bruce W Jentleson *Pipeline Politics: The Complex Political Economy of East–West Energy Trade.* Ithaca, N.Y: Cornell University Press, 1986.
8. *Atlanta Constitution*, October 24, 1988.
9. *Financial Times*, August 30, 1988.

10. See Gerald Segal 'In Europe, A Dissenting View on the Pacific Century', *International Herald Tribune*, September 6, 1988.

11. See, for example, David P Calleo *Beyond American Hegemony*. New York: Basic Books, 1988; and Paul Kennedy *The Rise and Fall of the Great Powers*. New York: Random House, 1987, especially pp. 517 ff.

12. Jean François-Poncet 'The European Pillar', *Atlantic Focus*, October 1987, p. 1.

13. *Ibid.*, p. 4.

14. *International Herald Tribune*, September 9, 1988.

CHAPTER 8

The Reagan Years:
A Retrospective

STEVE SMITH

There is a paradox about the Reagan years: an Administration that stressed the need for decisive leadership ended up bequeathing to its successor a set of issues that have to be addressed in the very near future. The most obvious of these is the budget deficit, but in this chapter the concern will be with the defence and foreign policy legacy. My claim will be that there are at least half a dozen areas in which President Bush has to make fundamental choices; these choices may well impact very severely on the European members of the NATO Alliance.

When President Reagan came to power in 1981, he seemed to symbolise something very different from his immediate predecessor. Where President Carter saw complexity, President Reagan saw simplicity; where Carter saw indigenous change, Reagan saw a manifestation of international communism; where Carter saw an increasingly multipolar and pluralist world, Reagan saw an essentially bipolar and realist world. For Carter, the problem was how to manage events in such a rapidly changing world; for Reagan the problem was less one of management, and more one of leadership. Nothing symbolised this more than the 444 day crisis of the American hostages in Iran. For many American citizens, the television pictures of the burned out helicopters in the Iranian desert following the abortive attempt to rescue the hostages in April 1980 summed up the Carter years. The United States no longer stood tall, could no longer determine world events, could be pushed around by virtually any power, and, above all, had been replaced by the Soviet Union as the number one power in the world. It matters not that these images were largely myths, only that this was a common perception and as such was one of the factors that led to the election of Ronald Reagan.

The first four years of his administration witnessed a very different public mood in the United States. Reagan spoke of the need to act decisively, to confront the Soviets, to stand firm on terrorism and to build up American defence strength so that the United States could impose its will when necessary. Yet, even in these heady days, there were a number of indications that there was a gap between public statements and policy implementation. By the time of the second term of the Administration, these gaps became more obvious, with the Iran–Contra scandal and the policy towards terrorism being the most clear-cut examples.

But as the transition between the Reagan and Bush Administrations takes place, it is useful to look in some detail at the defence and foreign policy arena to see whether this general theme can be substantiated. In short, what legacy has President Reagan left for his successor and does this inform our judgement of the central paradox of the Reagan years?

Before looking at the Reagan legacy, it is important that we place the Reagan years in some kind of a context, if only because there is a real lack of clarity concerning the extent of change that occurred under him. The most significant point to make is that the defence build-up that is usually portrayed as the Reagan build-up, in fact dates from the last two years of the Carter Administration. A rough indication of this comes from the percentage of Gross National Product [GNP] spent on defence in the Fiscal Years (FY) 1977 to 1989;

FY 1977	4.9%
FY 1978	4.7%
FY 1979	4.7%
FY 1980	5.0%
FY 1981	5.2%
FY 1982	5.8%
FY 1983	6.2%
FY 1984	6.0%
FY 1985	6.2%
FY 1986	6.3%
FY 1987	6.2%
FY 1988	5.9%
FY 1989	5.7%[1]

The *turn-around* in defence spending, therefore, came under the Carter Administration. However, what is more important is that the Reagan years witnessed a massive increase in the levels of spending devoted to defence. Whilst the reversal in the trend may have had its origins in the Carter Administration, the Reagan years saw considerable increases in the actual sums involved. For example, the percentage of federal spending devoted to defence declined from 25.5 per cent in FY 1975 to 22.5 per cent in FY 1980; in the last Fiscal Year of the Carter Administration [FY 1981] it rose to 23.0 per cent but over the next eight Fiscal Years it was 24.5 per cent [FY 1982], 25.4 per cent [FY 1983], 25.9 per cent [FY 1984], 25.9 per cent [FY 1985],

26.8 per cent [FY 1986], 27.3 per cent [FY 1987], 26.2 per cent [FY 1988], and 26.1 per cent [FY 1989].[2]

Another indicator is the actual expenditure on defence. In constant (1985) dollars ($ millions) the sums involved were:

FY 1976	$181,668
FY 1980	$191,336
FY 1981	$213,478
FY 1982	$239,978
FY 1983	$259,968
FY 1984	$271,028
FY 1985	$286,802[3]

A final indicator is the rate of real growth in the defence budget. From FY 1976 to FY 1985, the rates were:

FY 1976	−8.2%
FY 1977	1.9%
FY 1978	0.5%
FY 1979	4.0%
FY 1980	3.1%
FY 1981	4.8%
FY 1982	7.8%
FY 1983	7.3%
FY 1984	4.2%
FY 1985	9.5%[4]

What all this means is that the Reagan Administration may have inherited a trend of increasing defence spending but the sums that they invested in defence were of a different order of magnitude. To give just two examples of this contrast, the percentage of GNP devoted to defence in the four Carter years averaged 4.9 per cent, whereas in the first four Reagan years it averaged 6.05 per cent. Real growth in the defence budget during the Carter years averaged 3.1 per cent, in the first four Reagan years it averaged 7.2 per cent. In current dollars (millions), defence expenditure increased from $178,365 in FY 1981 to $286,802 in FY 1985, an increase of about 60 per cent.

Now, the point of presenting all this data is that it was this expenditure, along with the public rhetoric about standing tall, that was responsible for the public image of the Administration. My argument is that this massive expenditure on defence created an image of an Administration that had a clear view of where it was going, whereas in reality the expenditure did not reflect any consistent view of the most appropriate United States defence posture. The image of a military build-up was accurate, but it did not mean that there was an underlying logic to the weapon systems chosen, nor to the strategy that lay behind the choices.

The test for this assertion is to look at the Reagan legacy. After all, the Administration had eight years, at least the first four of which were accompanied by massive public support. It had the chance to get legislation through Congress and to develop a coherent strategy for the United States defence establishment. Yet, if one looks at the situation at the end of the Reagan Administration, there are a number of very problematic areas for the new Administration to deal with. I will look at six as exemplars of what I believe is a common feature of the Reagan legacy in all policy areas. Were this chapter to be written on any other policy arena I believe that the same broad conclusions would follow.

The *first* area concerns United States strategic forces, and there are three related aspects of this: the first relates to their composition; the second is the policy over strategic arms control: and the third is the conception of nuclear strategy underlying American weapons procurement.

With regard to the composition of United States strategic forces, it should be remembered that Reagan came to power arguing that the Carter years had been responsible for a serious decline in American strategic capability compared to the Soviet Union. The United States needed rearming, and, specifically, needed to match the Soviet's development in hard-target ICBM capability. This is precisely the message contained in the writings of the Committee on the Present Danger,[5] and reflected in Reagan's 1980 campaign speeches.

The record, however, has been very different. There has been a build-up, of course, but it has not resulted in either the force structure posited by Reagan or in any coherent policy regarding force structure. The most obvious example of this is that of the history of the American ICBM force under Reagan. Recollect that Reagan was a powerful critic of Carter's inability to make decisions on this aspect of defence policy. Yet the history of the ICBM force under Reagan is marked by exactly this lack of continuity and clarity.

Take, for example, the MX missile: originally justified by the United States Air Force (USAF) as a way of closing the window of vulnerability (itself now exposed as a myth).[6] Under the Carter Administration, it was to be deployed in a multiple protective shelter basing mode. At least this made strategic sense, given the nature of the problem. Yet, within a year of coming to power, Reagan had abandoned this basing mode. There then followed a period of considerable confusion as basing modes came and went. The interim choice, that of putting the first 50 missiles in old Minuteman II silos, was only possible after the President's Commission on Strategic Forces (known as the Scowcroft Commission), in its report of April 1983, announced that the window of vulnerability no longer existed.[7]

But even this decision did not allow the Administration to convince Congress that it had a clear idea of how MX fitted into the United States force structure. Only 50 of the 100 missiles called for by the Department of

Defense (DoD) were approved by Congress, the other 50 awaiting a basing mode that was acceptable to Congress. The current plan calls for these to be rail-garrisoned. The problem, of course, is that putting them in the very silos that were deemed to be so vulnerable as to require the development of the missile does not inspire confidence in the strategic policy of the Administration. This problem is exacerbated by the other main finding of the Scowcroft Commission, which was that the United States should overcome the eventual vulnerability of its ICBM force by developing and deploying a new single-warhead mobile ICBM—known as Midgetman (officially designated the small ICBM, or SICBM).[8] Since the report of the Commission was published, there has been enormous Congressional support for the Midgetman (resulting in it being known in Washington as Congressman), but much less support from the USAF, which sees it as a very expensive way of buying 500 warheads (since the costs of a 500 SICBM force, with hardened launchers, is far more than the cost of an extra 50 MXs each of which carries 10 warheads).

This has led to considerable budgetary confusion: for example, in the FY 1989 budget process, the Administration orginally asked for $800 million for MX rail-garrision research, leaving $200 million to keep the SICBM on ice. Yet in Congress these priorities were altered, with the House giving $600 million to the SICBM and only $100 million for MX; in the Senate the sums were $50 million to the SICBM and $700 million to the MX.[9] The eventual compromise was that Congress authorised $850 million for the ICBM force; of this, $250 million was for the MX, $250 million was for the SICBM, leaving $350 million for the new President, who had to make a report on his plans for the United States strategic force by February 1989.[10] In the event, President Bush chose to prolong the lives of both programmes, thereby avoiding a choice between them. At the time of writing (July 1989), he is still undecided about the future shape of the United States ICBM force. The problem is that no clear idea of what the US ICBM force should look like emerged during the Reagan Administration. Since, the choice has now to be made by President Bush.

The paradox, then, is that after spending vast sums on ICBM research and deployment, the United States has no integrated strategy for that force; it is still not clear what the mix of systems should be, how many MXs and how many SICBMs. Nor is it clear what mix of basing modes should be adopted. Most importantly, there is no agreement on the roles for mobile and fixed ICBMs, or for single warheaded and multiple warheaded ICBMs. This is really a major indictment of the strategic policy of the Reagan Administration. It has left ICBM development and deployment in a state of disarray and it is not at all clear what the force will look like at the end of the century. Some very difficult decisions had to be made and the Reagan Administration avoided making them.

A similar story can be told about the other areas of the strategic triad, most notably in the case of the manned bomber force, where the Administration has gone ahead with the procurement of a bomber, the B1, which was virtually obsolete by the time it was deployed. The same picture is found in the American ASAT programme. Nevertheless, the lack of direction for the ICBM programme remains the major problem. This is because it has had a clear limiting effect on the American START position. Indeed, it now seems likely that no START Treaty will emerge until the United States makes firm decisions about the future shape of its ICBM force. This lack of direction was reflected in the confusing negotiating positions taken by the United States at the START negotiations during the Reagan years. Nowhere is this clearer than in the area of mobile, single-warhead ICBMs. Here, the United States moved from a policy of encouraging their deployment in its build-down proposals in 1983 to a policy of proposing that they should be banned in 1985, because they were destabilising. In the last year of the Reagan Administration, this confusion extended to the role for SLCMs. The other obvious policy reversal came over the need for INF systems, where, despite the public statements, the rationale for the original deployment of GLCMs and Pershing 2 missiles was completely ignored in the rush for an arms control success.

Policy towards strategic arms control has also lacked coherence, although there has certainly been a continuity in the basic negotiating position if not the public statements.[11] On the one hand the Administration spoke of the desirability of constructing a strategic arms control environment with the Soviets, and was actively involved in negotiations with them for the bulk of its period of office. On the other, the arms control proposals made by the United States during this period tended to be unrealistic, if an agreement was the desired outcome. It has only been since the arrival of Mikhail Gorbachev to the leadership of the Soviet Union that there has been any progress on arms control, simply because his *perestroika* demands some arms control at the strategic level. For this reason, he has made significant shifts in the Soviet negotiating position, most notably over the Soviet heavy ICBM force. The result has been, much in the same way as occurred in the INF case, that the Soviets have accepted American proposals that were designed to prevent agreement. The second zero and the global ban on INF systems are examples in the INF case, and the Soviet concessions on the SS18, on throw-weight and on SDI research are examples of the START concessions. The Soviets' concession on the SS18 sub-limit has reversed a policy that they have stuck to for twenty years.

This Soviet concession is often presented by the American Administration as a justification for their tough stand over START, a direct result of standing firm. Yet this is misleading, since the reason for presenting demands over the Soviet heavy missiles was never simply that of a negotiating position, it was also something that it was felt would never be accepted by the Soviets. What is interesting to note is that, since the Soviet concession, progress over a START agreement has been slow. There were very few major obstacles to agreement remaining in the last of the Reagan years, yet the political will for such an agreement was not there. Of the five remaining areas of disagreement (the SS18 follow-on; the ICBM sublimit; SLCM sub-limits; restrictions on mobile ICBMs; and restrictions on ALCMs), none is so serious as to prevent a treaty being signed on its own. They are exactly the kind of issues that were successfully dealt with in the 'back channel' during SALT I and SALT II.

The justification of holding to a firm line in the START negotiations was, of course, the joint ones of obtaining concessions from the Soviets and wait-ing until the modernisation process had built up American forces to levels that allowed the United States to negotiate from strength. Yet even a cursory examination of the data reveals that the US–Soviet strategic balance shifted *away* from the United States during the Reagan years. This may not matter much, but it does indicate the gap between public utterances and reality. The criteria used by the President to show how the Soviets had gained a lead in the Carter years (missile warhead and launcher ratios) actually moved even more away from the United States during the very American build-up that was claimed gave the United States the possi-bility of negotiating from strength.

Not only this, but the Reagan Administration followed a very ambiguous line over arms control agreements to which the United States was a party. The 1974 and 1976 underground nuclear test threshold treaties were not ratified, despite the embarrassing fact that the Soviets proved that seismic sensors were sufficiently accurate to police the 150 kiloton threshold, whereas the American-favoured compliance system, CORRTEX, over-estimated an American test explosion in the 140 kiloton range by about 10–12 per cent (two American tests reportedly gave figures of 158 and 163 kilotons).[12]

The most obvious area of ambiguity concerned SALT II where, despite continuing to negotiate in the START forum, the United States announced it would no longer be bound by the terms of the SALT II Treaty in May 1986. Congressional action has meant that America has just stayed within the Treaty, although the Administration has continued to propose the deployment of more warheads than are allowed by one of the key quantita-tive sublimits of the Treaty.[13] It is paradoxical that the Administration has declared its intention to break the existing strategic framework whilst attacking the Soviets for their non-compliance in a series of highly publicised reports. In reality, whatever the Soviets have done, they have never broken anything like as important an element of the unratified Treaty as has the United States. In summary, there is little doubt that the Reagan Administration never wanted a START agreement, and that their policy of doubting Soviet compliance created an atmosphere in which any agreement that does result will have a very stormy ride through Congress over the issue of verification.

The final area of the Administration's strategic policy that was less than clear concerns nuclear strategy. There is no need to rehearse the vast debates over whether the Administration favoured a warfighting strategy; suffice it to say that it took decisions over the type of systems that would be deployed in the next decade which encouraged thoughts that the United States might be retreating from a commitment to a strictly second-strike posture. Developments in C^3I and in the ASAT area are good examples of this trend, as is the seeming determination to deploy the MX ICBM. Incautious statements by senior members of the Administration also encouraged the perception of the United States moving towards a policy of pre-emption.

On the other hand, the Administration, to the astonishment and alarm of European leaders, has been seen as moving away from a policy of reliance on nuclear weapons. Whether President Reagan actually said to Gorbachev at Reykjavik that he wanted to get rid of *all* nuclear weapons by 1996 can be debated; what cannot is that he did propose abolishing all nuclear-armed missiles. This indicated a sea-change in United States strategy, and gave European leaders massive cause for concern, fuelling fears of a withdrawal of the United States commitment to Europe. Together, these two developments left many wondering just what was the nuclear strategy of the United States.

Such a concern was also invoked by the policy of the Administration in the *second* area with which we are concerned, that of the policy towards SDI and the ABM Treaty. As the Reagan Administration left office, it was by no means clear what was the fate of the SDI programme. There seemed to be agreement that the costs and likely ineffectiveness of the systems would ensure that there was no large scale deployment of defensive systems in space. However, all this is supposition since the Administration had not taken any of the critical political decisions that were necessary. These three items were left to the Bush Administration.

Having announced the research programme in 1983, President Reagan continued to support the programme throughout his term of office. In FY 1984–1989, about $16.2 billion was spent on SDI research, but this did not enable the Administration to make decisions over the shape of any future defensive system. Whilst SDI successfully weathered the hardware debates of the first few years, it proved less successful in overcoming criticisms that it faced fundamental problems over its software and battle-management capabilities. Similar problems have arisen over its effectiveness. Together, these seem likely to make the deployment of anything approaching a full-scale system unlikely. In terms of the software problems, the resignation of David Parnas from the SDIO computing support panel in June 1985 signalled that there was some doubt as to the possible effectiveness of the software needed. This doubt has continued, notwithstanding the report of the SDIO's computing support group (known as the Eastport Study Group) to the contrary. This is so serious a problem that the United States Office of

Technology Assessment concluded in May 1988, after access to classified material, that: 'there would be a significant probability . . . that the first (and presumably only) time the BMD system were used in a real war, it would suffer a catastrophic failure'.[14] In OTA's view, this was not a problem that could be resolved in the foreseeable future, since it related not so much to a technological problem as to a generic limitation on the reliability of large-scale computer systems in the absence of operational testing.

Even ignoring this problem, the latest estimates are that it would not be until the end of the 1990s that the first phase of SDI defences could be deployed, and not until about 2010 when exotic techniques could begin to serve as weapons. In short, whatever could be deployed before the end of this century would use kinetic kill systems (such as ERIS, HEDI, and the SBI), and not the exotic laser and particle-beam weapons conjured up by the President's original discussions of the plan. Yet, the Administration continued to talk publicly as if the proposal would involve exotic technology. Not only this but the evidence seems clear that the early phases of SDI will be very ineffective. One study gives an estimated overall effectiveness of 16 per cent.[15] This is at variance with the picture of the effectiveness of SDI painted by the Administration, and, more importantly, implies a very different role for SDI than that envisaged by the President in his original speech. Put simply, SDI will never replace deterrence, it will never provide the means of making nuclear weapons (even ballistic missile launched missiles) 'impotent and obsolete'.

The problem is not so much that specialists and allied governments are not aware of this picture but rather that the emerging consensus on the likely future for SDI was not reflected in the official policy of the Reagan Administration. They continued to pay lip-service to a version of SDI that was no longer considered possible in the scientific community. The likelihood is that President Bush will quietly cut back on SDI research whilst not being able publicly to abandon the programme. Yet, the Reagan Administration delayed any decisions over the timetable for early deployment, despite the pressure for such a decision from the DoD, whilst continuing to request sizeable sums for continued research across the board. Policymaking has effectively been carried out by the SDIO's budgetary process.

Not only will President Bush have to make some overdue decisions over the future of SDI, but he will also have to sort out the Administration's policy over the ABM Treaty. At the same time as it was attacking the Soviets for breaching the Treaty by building the LPAR at Krasnoyarsk, the Administration was itself engaged in a questionable act of compliance by modernising (or building?) its early warning radars at Thule and Fylingdales. One can debate whether either of these American and Soviet moves were compliant with the Treaty, but of greater significance is the fact that the United States announced a reinterpretation of the ABM Treaty in October 1985. Under this interpretation, the United States was allowed to test, but not deploy, exotic BMD systems. This interpretation was very quickly discredited, and the Administration undertook to maintain the existing interpretation. But the damage was done. Since then, the Administration used the Krasnoyarsk issue by threatening to declare it as a material breach of the Treaty, thereby allowing the United States to withdraw from the conditions of the Treaty without having to abrogate it. There was certainly considerable speculation in the press in the summer of 1988 that the DoD was proposing declaring Krasnoyarsk a material breach, thereby allowing the United States to be free to test exotics as part of the SDI programme. That the Administration did not accept this view does not mean that it is at all clear what its view of the Treaty was. President Bush will have to clarify his Administration's policy on this.

The final issue within the general area of defensive systems is that the Reagan Administration never clarified its view of the most healthy and stabilising relationship between offensive and defensive systems. The implication of the President's SDI speech and of the expenditure of such sums on the research programme has been that the Administration favoured a mixture of defensive and offensive systems. However, it remains unclear just what such a mixture would look like and what kinds of mixtures would be most stabilising. In short, the worry was that the Administration was allowing technology to lead policy, in much the same way as occurred with the development of MIRV in the 1960s. As Henry Kissinger remarked about MIRV, he wished that he had thought through the consequences of a world in which both superpowers had MIRVed ICBMs. Perhaps the same could be said for the current situation of the mix between offence and defence. The upshot is that a whole set of decisions will have to be made about the future of the research programme as well as the new Administration's commitment to the ABM Treaty régime. The Reagan Administration has bequeathed a very confused, ambiguous and contradictory legacy to President Bush in this area.

The *third* area that will be examined is that of the American commitment to Europe in the wake of the INF Treaty. The problems are easy to state: will the United States continue to maintain the level of forces that it has done since the 1950s? How will the United States react to the sweeping conventional reductions proposed by Gorbachev in December 1988? What will Washington do over Soviet proposals for a third zero option in battlefield nuclear forces? By the end of 1988, burden sharing was already rearing its head in the policy debates in the United States and this (as earlier chapters have shown) looks like being the most prominent issue within NATO for the next decade. These issues all require fairly immediate attention by the new President, but for my purposes the more important point is that since the INF Treaty, the Reagan Administration failed to construct a coherent or integrated policy towards NATO. The problem exists because President Reagan desired an arms control success so much that he turned on its head the original rationale for the deployment of GLCMs and Pershing 2 missiles. Removing them, even in exchange for Soviet SS20s, has done nothing to calm European fears about coupling. The Treaty implies that American nuclear forces are in Europe to counter Soviet nuclear forces; this logic leads to a set of similarly mutual reduction packages which, whilst being equal in numerical terms, do not match the realities of the process of consensus formation in NATO.

The Reagan Administration, therefore, acted in a way that created problems for the Alliance, and the unfolding logic of events will provide a difficult agenda for President Bush. The situation at the end of the Reagan years can only be described as one of confusion. The process leading up to the signature of the INF Treaty had concerned many European leaders, a concern fuelled by the President's own acceptance at Reykjavik that ballistic missiles could be dispensed with altogether. Burden sharing looks like the name of the game for the next few years, especially given the background of rising United States protectionism and the possibility of a trade war between the United States and the European Community. It seems very unlikely that the Europeans will be able significantly to increase any contributions they make to the defence of Europe, and this portends confrontation and disagreement.

The policy of the new Administration to the role of American forces in Europe will be exacerbated by the *fourth* area to be considered, which is that of the severe budget deficit in the United States. The problem is that the Reagan Administration presided over a dramatic worsening in three central budgetary areas, the trade balance, the national debt, and the federal budget deficit. Of these the latter two are particularly relevant for defence. When President Reagan came to office, the federal budget deficit was $78 billion; by 1985 it was $221 billion; by 1988 it was $150 billion. In 1980 the national debt was $989 billion; by 1985 it was $2.6 trillion, and it is predicted to rise to $3.5 trillion by 1995, even assuming that the federal budget is balanced according to the Gramm-Rudman-Hollings amendment. More significantly, the percentage of federal spending that is required to meet the interest payments on the national debt increased from 7 per cent in 1980 to 14 per cent by 1988, and is forecast to rise to 16 per cent by 1995.[16]

These figures indicate the most serious problem facing the new President: he has to find some way of reducing the federal budget deficit, and this will have likely implications for the defence budget. This is because he is required, by Gramm–Rudman, to reduce the deficit by increasing amounts, so that it is balanced by 1995. In FY 1990 the maximum figure for the deficit will be $110 billion. Now, the likely deficit for that year is estimated to be around $140 billion. The problem for defence is that the vast bulk of the federal budget is fixed, and cannot be cut in any immediate way: of the FY 1989 federal budget of approximately $1.1 trillion, the rough proportions are—28 per cent defence; 25 per cent social security; 14 per cent interest payments on the national debt; 10 per cent medicare/medicaid; 10 per cent other entitlements. Within these totals, the unavoidables in the budget total about 78 per cent—composed of 19 per cent on contracts (mostly in defence), 25 per cent social security, 14 per cent interest on the debt, 10 per cent medicare/medicaid, and 10 per cent on other entitlements. This implies that the new Administration will have to look hard at the remaining 22 per cent of the budget to find the necessary savings, given the new President's 'read my lips' pledge over tax increases. This must mean serious constraints on the defence budget, but even there the sums that could be easily saved are very small. For example, scrapping *all* SDI research would save no more than $4 billion; bringing 100,000 troops home from Europe could save only $4.6 billion, and then only if they were disbanded; halting all spending on any new ICBM would save only $850 million in FY 1989, and cancelling the SICBM plans would only save $29 billion, *in the lifetime* of the missile. In short, the savings that are needed in the short term, for example the $30 billion or so needed for FY 1990, are far greater than can be obtained from the defence budget. This implies that the budget will be squeezed, because there are few other obvious sources for savings, and also that the squeeze will be applied for the foreseeable future. The picture for defence spending is that real cuts will be likely. Although there has been some press speculation that has mentioned figures of $360 billion cuts in defence over four years, this is out of the question. More likely is a small progressive cut in defence spending, which will require critical decisions to be made over procurement plans and over the shape of the defence establishment. President Bush's budget proposals envisage, at best, an essentially static defence budget, representing real cuts in defence spending. The budget deficit is the most serious problem facing the new President, and it will provide the backdrop to his Administration. It will require major decisions to be made over defence, and this will create a sense of uncertainty and flux in alliance defence planning. This problem over the budget deficit was created by the Reagan Administration and literally set the agenda for the new Administration; as such it has constrained the choices that could be made, and it calls for urgent decisions. This is the most important legacy of the Reagan years, reflecting a policy of financing a military build-up on borrowed money while, at the same time, paying lip-service to the goal of balancing the budget.

The remaining two areas to be discussed are much more general than those covered thus far. They can be simply and briefly noted. The *fifth* area concerns the attitude of the Reagan Administration to the use of force. The Administration projected American military power more than was the case in the Carter years, but its record of success was very poor. The introduction of the Marines into Beirut is but the clearest example of that, but even with such 'successes' as Grenada, the bombing of Libya, and the introduction of naval forces into the Gulf, there remains a doubt over the long-term effects of such actions. Not only might these backfire in the next few years (and the bombing of the Pan Am jumbo in December 1988 is an example of this) but there might also be an unfortunate effect on the United States' allies. Their publics may see America as too dangerous an ally to be too closely aligned with. President Reagan's 'Rambo' image certainly led to the United States being seen by many in Europe as a greater threat to world peace than the Soviets in the mid-1980s. This could undermine the Alliance from within, especially with a friendly and personable leader in the Kremlin. The legacy with regards to the projection of United States force is, therefore, rather mixed, and the new President has had to think about what the role of United States force should be.

The *sixth* area focuses on the other superpower. The central problem is that President Reagan came to office denouncing the Soviets, and left office with US–Soviet relations in a very different state. Yet this has been something to do with concerns about the history books, and much more to do with the arrival of Gorbachev, than it has been to any strategy of the Reagan Administration. There has been no clear discussion of what the United States wants from the Soviets or about the role that the Soviets should play in world politics, let alone about the kind of Soviet Union the United States would like to see. American policy has been reactive. Gorbachev has seized and held on to the initiative, and it has often seemed as if Washington was totally unable to respond to his statements and proposals. This has led to many seeing the United States as negative, and lacking any sense of purpose and direction. There has been a policy vacuum and Bush will have to fill it.

In all these policy areas, the Reagan Administration left office leaving behind it confusion and contradictions. Major policy decisions have now to be made in each, and these will have significant effects on the NATO Alliance. The problem has been that the Reagan years saw a lot of sound and imagery but little in the way of action. Public statements were unusually unreliable guides to policy, and there was usually massive contradictions within policies. With his eye on his domestic audience, the President often implied one thing and did another. There was a lack of consultation with the allies and a real lack of continuity in policy. Above all, the President avoided taking a set of critical decisions, preferring instead to allow policy to drift. Hard choices were not made, with the President instead giving the impression that there was real coherence and a real determination behind American policy. The reality is very different: for the Reagan years were essentially wasted years in which the arms race has been given new dimensions and in which billions of dollars have been spent on the symbols of an active foreign and defence policy which all too often was contradictory and ill thought-out.

The paradox with which I started this chapter is, I believe, supported in each of the six areas I have examined. The new Administration has to make a decision over the future of the ICBM force, until which time there can be no finalization of a START agreement. It must also make a set of other procurement decisions, decisions that will be especially difficult given the budget deficit. Similar immediate choices have to be made in the area of conventional reductions in Europe and over post-INF nuclear agreements in Europe. The new President also faces difficult decisions over SDI, especially as the first tests that threaten the ABM Treaty are scheduled for 1990 and 1991.

The picture, then, is one of the new President facing an immediate agenda containing several critical and complex problems, each of which will require policy choices in the first year of his Administration. The problem is that this agenda has been drawn up by his predecessor, and drawn up not by choice but by omission and by a lack of leadership. As we have seen, the Reagan years were, surprisingly, years of neglect in the area of American defence policy. Style replaced substance, fantasy replaced realism, and the statement that policy was being made all too often was the policy. The lack of leadership, the concern with image and the avoidance of critical decisions has left the new Administration to make crucial policy decisions in the areas of START, the US ICBM force, the B-2 bomber, SDI, conventional arms control, ASAT, battlefield nuclear agreements, and the ABM Treaty. These all landed on the President's desk in the first few months of his Administration. In the medium term, he will have to decide on his policy over the use of force, and, more importantly, on his Soviet policy. Underlying all of these will be his attempts to deal with the American budget deficit. The acid test will be how much of his first, and possibly only, term of office will President Bush have to devote to making the critical decisions that should have been made in the Reagan years.

Notes

1. See *Report of the Secretary of Defense Frank C Carlucci to the Congress, on the Fiscal Year 1989 Budget.* Washington, DC: Government Printing Office, 1988, p. 299.
2. *Ibid.*
3. Data obtained from *ibid.*, p. 297, and John Collins *US–Soviet Military Balance 1980–1985.* Washington, DC: Pergamon-Brassey's, 1985, p. 296.
4. See, Collins, *op. cit.*, p. 301.
5. These are collected in Charles Tyroler (ed), *Alerting America.* Washington, DC: Pergamon-Brassey's, 1984.
6. See Steve Smith 'MX and the Vulnerability of American Missiles', *ADIU Report*, Volume 4(1), 1982, pp. 1–5; and Steve Smith 'Problems of Assessing Missile Accuracy', *RUSI Journal*, Volume 130(4), 1985, pp. 35–40.
7. See, *Report of the President's Commission on Strategic Forces.* Washington, DC: 1983, p. 17.
8. *Ibid.*, pp. 14–16.
9. See *Arms Control Today*, July/August 1988, p. 27.
10. See *Ibid.*, November 1988, pp. 27, 29.
11. These negotiations are discussed in Strobe Talbott *Deadly Gambits.* New York: Knopf, 1984, and Strobe Talbott *The Master of the Game.* New York: Knopf, 1988, pp. 185–394.
12. See *Arms Control Today*, October 1988, p. 26.

13. The US currently has 1368 'MIRVed' launchers, 48 more than allowed by the Treaty, but the FY 1989 budget legislation passed by Congress called for two Poseidon submarines to be withdrawn from service and to be tied up at dockside, thereby keeping the number of launchers in service within the Treaty's requirements. However, technically, even this method of trying to keep the US within the terms of the agreement fails, since tying the submarines up in dock does not count as a way of dismantling them under the Treaty. See *Arms Control Today*, November 1988, p. 29.

14. Office of Technology Assessment, *SDI: Technology, Survivability and Software*. Washington, DC: Government Printing Office, May 1988, p. 4.

15. See the unpublished report written for Senators William Proxmire and J Bennett Johnston by Douglas Waller and James Bruce, *SDI: Progress and Challenges Part Two*, March 19, 1987, p. ii.

16. These figures were presented by Stan Collender of Price Waterhouse Office of Government Services at an Oxford Analytica seminar in Oxford, September 21–24 1988.

CHAPTER 9

Burden Sharing: The Evolution of the French Defence Policy Since 1981

GUY de CARMOY

In a book, published a few months before his election to the Presidency of the Republic, François Mitterrand observed: 'There is antinomy between the strategy based on the sole defence of the national sanctuary and the strategy based on the Alliance'.[1]

The French defence posture as set up by de Gaulle is well known. France remains a member of the Atlantic Alliance but disengaged in 1966 from the NATO integrated command. Nuclear deterrence is limited to the 'vital interests' of the country, which maintains its freedom of decision in the field of defence.

According to the 1958 Constitution, the President plays an important role as Head of the Armed Forces. This role has been enhanced since French nuclear weapons became operational. The President decides on the use or on the threat of use of these weapons. President Mitterrand, since his election, has shown a specific interest in defence matters.

The question is therefore to what extent François Mitterrand has been willing to reduce the antinomy he rightly denounced. To answer this question, one should consider three closely interrelated aspects of French defence policy in the 1980s: Franco–German relations, Franco–NATO relations and lastly the prospects for a so-called European pillar in the Atlantic Alliance.

Franco–German Relations

Franco–German relations in the field of defence are hampered by two major obstacles. First, France is a nuclear power and West Germany is not. Second, France is out of NATO's integrated command and West Germany is the main continental partner of NATO.

The French motivations for a military rapprochement between the two countries are, on the one hand, the strengthening of the ties beween the Federal Republic and the West and on the other the growing conviction that the defence of France cannot be assured by French forces alone.

Several positive steps have been taken to tighten bilateral defence relations, sometimes hampered by setbacks.

In 1982, President Mitterrand proposed the creation of a Franco–German Committee on Defence and Security, as a late implementation of the Franco–German Treaty of 1963, the military clauses of which had remained dormant. Thus regular consultations took place on strategy and procurement. In the same year, France created the Rapid Action Force (FAR), a highly mobile military unit, equipped with armoured vehicles and with helicopters. It was intended to convey the French determination to operate immediately and effectively in the defence of the West German territory.[2] This force depended on NATO for logistical support.

In January 1983, on the occasion of the 20th Anniversary of the 1963 Treaty, François Mitterrand, in a speech at the Bundestag, expressed his views in favour of the deployment in West Germany of the US Pershing II and Cruise missiles. In so doing, he was encouraging the West German Government to implement a resolution of the Atlantic Council. This move therefore was both in the direction of NATO and in the direction of the Christian Democrat and Liberal coalition. Mitterrand managed to establish close personal relations with Chancellor Helmut Kohl, notwithstanding diverging domestic political leanings.

In order to allay German concerns about the use of French tactical nuclear weapons on West German territory, Mitterrand, in a joint statement with Kohl in February 1986, announced that France would consult with West Germany before taking such a step.

A first Franco–German joint military exercise took place in Bavaria in September 1987 under the name of *Moineau Hardi*. This exercise was consonant with Chancellor Kohl's June 1987 proposal, seconded by President Mitterrand, to form an experimental Franco–German army brigade. Both countries decided at the same time to establish a joint defence council. The first meeting took place on 20 May 1989. The garrisons of the brigade, which comprises two regiments of the French Rapid Action Force, are to be located in the south of the Federal Republic.[3]

Against this succession of positive actions pertaining to consultation and to specific troop movements, one should mention negative steps. In the field of arms procurement, in 1982 the two countries failed to reach an agreement on building a common tank. Talks started in 1983 on a multilateral proposal for the construction of a European Combat Aircraft. After a lengthy internal debate, France opted out of the project in 1985. One reason was a disagreement on the type of plane to be built. The French wanted a close support aircraft, the other parties, including the Germans, a long-range fighter.

A second reason pertained to considerations of employment in the French aircraft industry and especially in the Dassault firm. Marcel Dassault wanted to be the exclusive leader of the works and his views prevailed, at a considerable development cost, according to a recently disclosed parliamentary report. Nonetheless, the construction of the plane named *Rafale* will be pursued.[4] By contrast, the two countries decided to engage in the construction of a combat helicopter. A psychological mistake was made by the French command when they decided not to invite NATO authorities to the 1987 Franco–German exercise in Bavaria.

In 1986, François Mitterrand had written an introduction to his collected speeches in which he stated bluntly 'Germany belongs to Europe, for without Germany there is no Europe'.[5] In a December 1987 interview with *Le Nouvel Observateur*, he dealt with the global subject of the strategy of France, and expressed his ambition to develop with West Germany 'an embryo of a common army of a conventional type and to co-operate in view of a common defence'. Mitterrand endorsed Jacques Chirac's statement (in his then capacity of Prime Minister) that 'there cannot be a battle of Germany and a battle of France'. But he stressed that the President of the Republic was judge of the moment when the aggression against West Germany would threaten France's 'vital interests'. He confirmed that the ultimate nuclear warning—which is not proper to short term weapons—'would not be delivered on the German territory'.[6]

In a July 1988 interview, Jean-Pierre Chevènement, the new Defence Minister, stated that France wanted 'to build with West Germany a real community of fate' and that 'obviously the security space of France did not start on the Rhine'.[7]

To what extent do the French attitudes in favour of a bilaterial defence satisfy the requirements of the Federal Republic? France has accepted the view that a battle for West Germany would define the conditions of a battle for France. The FRG would like France to participate in the forward strategy, to give preference to deterrence over a battle in Europe and to stress the automatic character of its defence commitments.

On the first point, the location of the FAR and the planned location of a Franco–German brigade operating in West Germany may be interpreted as steps in the direction of a forward strategy in the conventional field. The Platform of the West European Union (WEU) adopted in November 1987 mentions that the signatories will 'provide for the defence of the borders' of its member states.

The increase in the range of the French tactical weapons, both land-based and airborne, will reinforce deterrence. The *Hadès* missile due to be operational in 1992 will have a range close to 500 kilometres. The ASMP could be transported by a Mirage 2000 N, this target could be substantially expanded beyond the borders of West Germany.[8] This would take into account the basic preoccupations of West German public opinion.

France certainly shares with West Germany the preference given to deterrence over an actual battle to be fought on the soil of Western Europe. In the words of President Mitterrand, 'the purpose of the strategy of deterrence is to prevent war, not to win it'.[9] What the Germans desire is to be informed of the French nuclear objectives as much as they are informed of the British nuclear objectives, through the Nuclear Planning Group (NPG) of NATO.

The Germans are not asking for an explicit nuclear coverage, but they wish France to assert its automatic defence commitment as soon as the Elbe is crossed.[10] Such a commitment is in conformity with the 1954 Paris Treaty which created the Western European Union. France has not taken such a formal commitment because it insists on the independence of its decision in case of war.[11] Nonetheless, André Giraud, the former French defence minister, attempted to give a wider interpretation of the concept of 'vital interests' which should take into consideration the political, economic and cultural ties linking France to its neighbours.[12]

Lastly, it is in this area of conventional forces that West Germany expects France to make a contribution to its defence, as the demographic decline in Germany will have an impact on the potential strength of its forces in the 1990s. But in her 1987–1991 defence programme, adopted by an overwhelming majority of 536 votes to 35, France has given priority to modernising the submarine launched ballistic missiles. Appropriation for nuclear forces and for space amounting to 34 per cent of the programme, entirely devoted to equipment.[13]

The debate on arms control between the Great Powers, to be discussed hereafter, revealed significant reactions in French public opinion regarding defence. According to an April 1987 poll, 69 per cent of the people consulted considered that France was not able to assume its defence single-handed, thereby expressing their support for their Atlantic Alliance; 74 per cent stated that France should provide its help to a threatened ally; 63 per cent thought that French conventional forces should be engaged in the defence of West Germany; 88 per cent favoured the setting up of a common European defence.[14] Thus the poll clearly underlined the connection between Franco–German relations, Franco–NATO relations and the concept of a European defence.

Two respected defence experts, Helmut Sonnenfeld and Christoph Bertram, believe that Franco–German agreements are a camouflage for real French rapprochement with the Atlantic Alliance[15]—a view contested in French official circles.

Franco–NATO Relations

The relations between France and NATO have improved under the

Mitterrand presidency. Signs of Alliance solidarity have multiplied. Practical measures of co-operation have been adopted. France had to adjust to the changes in American military doctrine and strategy, which moved from the deployment of new arms in Western Europe to the conclusion of an arms control agreement with the Soviet Union. Nonetheless, the basic French doctrine remained formally unchanged, if subject to partial reinterpretation.

The President was keen to show publicly that France was an active and dedicated member of the Alliance. He proposed, for the first time since 1966, that the 1983 Summit meeting of the Atlantic Alliance should be held in Paris. At the May 1983 Summit of the larger Western countries in Williamsburg, President Mitterrand co-signed a declaration in which the security of the West was termed 'indivisible'. An important NATO summit meeting took place in Brussels in March 1988 in the light of the approval by the Allies of the December 1987 agreement between the United States and the Soviet Union on the reduction of Intermediate Nuclear Forces (INF) and more generally on the steps to be taken towards disarmament. The session was attended both by President François Mitterrand and by Prime Minister Jacques Chirac.

A number of measures underlined the burgeoning technical co-operation between France and the NATO integrated command. Thus, France's Air Force, always dependent on NATO for radar intelligence, purchased AWACS electronic surveillance planes in 1987. The French Navy, which used NATO codes, bought American electronic and communication gear. Authorisation was given to American troops to train in France and a first combat exercise for marines took place in South-West France. In January 1988, France recommitted itself to open its territory to NATO reinforcements, implying the use of ports to land on the continent.

In February 1989, French experts participated in the planning of the Alliance's future Air Control and Communications System (ACCS). If the negotiations come to fruition, this would mean a significant expansion of France's operational ties with NATO. But the French participation should be consonant with her independent position within the Alliance, stated the Defence Minister Pierre Chevènement in June 1989. In the same month, in the related field of telecommunications, a French company, Thomson CSF, was chosen as technical manager for NATO's Multifunction Information Distribution System (NIDS).[16]

There is growing realisation among some French experts that the concept of the sanctuary has vanished and that Europe is a priority. Therefore 'if France wants to influence the course of events, it must participate in the work of NATO'.[17] However this interpretation of strategic doctrine is not officially endorsed.

Mention has been made under the paragraph of Franco–German Relations of President Mitterrand's speech in January 1983 at the Bundestag.

The President explained that the maintenance of a balance of forces between the two alliances required a NATO response to the nuclear arms aimed at the European allies and specifically to the Soviet SS20. France therefore supported the deployment of Cruise missiles and Pershing IIs in West Germany. The American missiles were deployed from 1984 on.

Arms control negotiations started in January 1985 and developed in scope and speed in 1986–1987. In March 1987 President Mitterrand approved the principle of the negotiations between the two great powers on the Intermediate Nuclear Forces (INF). He stressed that French armaments were not an issue in the talks. He observed that the central nuclear systems of both powers were not concerend either, so that the deterrence between them would remain intact.[18]

In his interview with *Le Nouvel Observateur* of December 1987 mentioned above, the President commented on the recently signed Washington Treaty between the United States and the Soviet Union and on coupling between the United States and its European allies. On the Treaty he said: 'As the Americans and Russians have agreed to eliminate, under mutual control, SS20s and Pershing IIs, I can only approve them'. In his view, coupling has never been automatic. The American commitment is dependent upon the feeling that the United States, a world power, has stated that it cannot, without endangering itself, loosen its interest in Europe. As for France, it will preserve its nuclear deterrence capacity, whatever threat may bear on the integrity and independence of the country.[19]

At the March 1988 Atlantic Council in Brussels, France joined in the official approval of the December 1987 Washington Treaty. In his 'Letter to all the French' of April 1988, prior to his re-election as President of the Republic, Mitterrand wrote 'It is upstream of a war that our strategy lies, not downstream, there is for France no possible flexible response'.[20]

French analysts are not as negative as the President regarding flexible response and therefore express reservations on the Washington Treaty. François de Rose is of the opinion that, without joining NATO, France might participate in some of its works; he is suggesting that the strategic questions be put on the agenda of the Atlantic Council, of which France is a member.[21] The two stronger critics of the INF treaty are Pierre Lellouche and Pierre Gallois. Lellouche sees in the elimination of long-range (1000–5000 kilometre) and short-range (500–1000 kilometre) missiles i.e. in the so-called double zero option, 'a contract of mutual sanctuarisation passed by the superpowers to the detriment of the Europeans'.[22] Gallois asserts that President Reagan's criticism of nuclear arms, described as obsolete, played into the hands of the peace movement, especially in West Germany, thus supporting Soviet propaganda.[23] Both fear that an irresistible triple zero option—eliminating the theatre missiles (with a range of under 500 kilometres) would lead to a total denuclearisation of Western Europe.

The issue of the location and characteristics of American short-ranged nuclear weapons in West Germany raised a debate both in NATO circles and the German political arena. At the Atlantic Alliance Summit in March 1987, Chancellor Kohl reaffirmed the need to maintain American nuclear arms in Europe and his rejection of the triple-zero option. However, his critics at home called first for the elimination of all short-ranged missiles and later asked for urgent talks between the United States and the Soviet Union on the modernisation or replacement of the aged short-ranged *Lance* missiles. The German Government was inclined to begin negotiations soon on all short-ranged nuclear arms, including *Lance*. The United States and Britain were opposed to such talks. President François Mitterrand, at his press conference on 18 May 1989, backed the German Government in its desire to postpone talks about nuclear modernisation until 1992 but rejected West Germany's call for the United States to start early negotiations on short-ranged weapons. He added: 'This is not the time for a third zero option, far from it'.

In an important speech delivered in October 1988 at the Institute for Superior Studies of National Defence, President Mitterrand developed his concepts in the field of defence. His basic statement was that France should not refrain from possessing any of the arms retained by other powers. But he stressed that France should maintain its means in a state of sufficiency as opposed to the state of overarmament of the Superpowers. Strategic and pre-strategic weapons could not be divorced. The ultimate warning of the latter weapons should only be delivered on strictly military targets. France alone could judge where her 'vital interests' lay. These interests could be located outside her borders. Mitterrand added that France should be associated to the indispensable task of disarmament. He referred to the conditions he had set in his 1983 speech at the United Nations, namely a considerable reduction in the strategic armaments of the superpowers and the correction of the conventional imbalances.[24]

Conventional forces disarmament has been discussed unsuccessfully for many years in Vienna between the representatives of both the NATO countries and the Warsaw Pact countries. France had strongly opposed the principle of what she called bloc-to-bloc talks. The discussion resumed since the signature of the 1987 Washington Treaty on nuclear disarmament. President Mitterrand, being aware that the slow pace of conventional disarmament might weaken Chancellor Kohl's centre-right coalition and strengthen neutralist sentiment in Germany, decided that France would participate at all levels of disarmament discussions, including those on conventional forces.[25]

Addressing the United Nations General Assembly on 29 September 1988, President Mitterrand took another step regarding disarmament. With a view to halting the spread of chemical warfare, he proposed that an international conference should meet in Paris to reinvigorate the 1925 Geneva Convention against the use of chemical and bacteriological arms in war—a convention of which France is the depository. In so doing he was supporting the proposal made by President Reagan in the same setting a few days earlier. He suggested that chemical arms factories and stocks be put under international surveillance before being destroyed.[26]

The remarks on the reinterpretation of French strategy presented at the end of the paragraph on Franco–German relations apply necessarily to Franco–NATO relations. The President has repeatedly stated that France will not return to the NATO integrated command and will keep to itself the decision to use or threaten to use its nuclear armoury. But he has adopted a number of measures of technical co-operation with NATO and supported the 1987 Washington Treaty on arms control. Other significant trends concern an enlarged conception of the 'vital interests' of France, limitations in the use of tactical nuclear weapons on German territory and proposals for disarmament. Do these steps mean that the formula of a European Pillar in the Atlantic Alliance does have some substance, or at least some future?

France and the European Pillar

The debate on burden sharing and on more or less veiled threats of partial American troop withdrawals from Western Europe have fed a discussion on Western Europe's strategic role in the Alliance and on the possible creation of a 'European Pillar', an expression coined by President John F. Kennedy. This is not the place for an in-depth analysis of this concept but it is usual to evaluate the present scope of intra-European defence co-operation and the role played by France in such a co-operation, as distinct from direct Franco–German and Franco–NATO relations. This evaluation will help formulate some remarks on the nature of a possible European Pillar.

Intra-European defence co-operation can be considered in terms of institutions, of burden sharing and of co-operation between the two West European atomic powers.

Western European Union (WEU) is the sole specifically European defence institution. Its membership comprises seven member states all engaged on the Central Front of NATO (although Spain and Portugal have recently joined). The defence of the Northern Flank of NATO and that of the Southern Flank in the East of the Mediterranean (Greece and Turkey), remain essentially under American protection, WEU is a forum where resolutions are debated; it is not an instrument for action.

In 1985 the share in NATO defence expenditure of the three major West European states—Britain, France and West Germany—was quite substantial in relation to the share of the ten other West European NATO members 24.8 per cent as opposed to 13.3 per cent, but it was small in relation to the share of the United States, 61.5 per cent, it being observed that the United States also has defence responsibilties outside Europe and the Mediterranean in the Caribbean, the Middle East and the Pacific.[27]

Franco–British co-operation in the nuclear field is limited to co-ordinating overhaul schedules for ballistic missiles submarines. Mrs. Thatcher objected to Franco–British co-operation in the field of targeting on the ground that France was not a member of NATO.

Such are the facts as of today. What might be the role of a European Pillar tomorrow both in the field of conventional and of nuclear arms and what are the political constraints for such a role?

Presently there is no common market in Western Europe for conventional arms, nor an adequate standardisation. The Single European Act provides for the application of the common external tariff to armaments. This provision together with the implementation of the 1992 common market goal may help the European Community to bring greater efficiency in European weapons procurement. Trade creation effects by the large market, leading to higher economic growth may induce some European countries to increase their defence spending in response to the American demands on burden sharing.

The nuclear face of a future European Pillar is subject to a number of constraints and to differing evaluations. It is generally accepted that Western Europe must have a system of defence including nuclear arms. In the view of most analysts, NATO is very much a nuclear pact under United States leadership. The West Germans have more confidence in the American extended deterrence than in the British or the French minimum deterrent forces. 'As long as West European governments regard nuclear deterrence by American forces as essential for their security, there cannot be a European Pillar to support the Atlantic structure'.[28] What then is the actual value of the United States nuclear deterrence? According to Edward N. Luttwak 'the unreality of extended deterrence by the United States has gradually been exposed', essentially because of change in American attitudes and American perspectives.[29] Whether the negative views of Luttwak are confirmed or not, Western Europe cannot dispense with American protection in the form the United States is prepared to give it. The question is what the Europeans are able or prepared to do on their own.

The first constraint is that West Germany does not accept that tactical weapons can be fired by its allies on targets in its own territory (and also in the territory of East Germany). A second constraint is that flexible response is the only strategy acceptable to the Federal Republic of Germany. A third constraint is that the minimum deterrent forces of Britain and France are following different strategies—flexible response in the case of Britain, massive retaliation, after a last warning, in the case of France. How is it possible, in the circumstances, for Western Europe to have some sort of extended deterrence of its own capable of threatening Soviet territory? One would have to 'Europeanise' the French nuclear doctrine in order to establish a degree of Franco–British nuclear co-operation acceptable to West Germany. A suggestion has been made to this effect, consisting in the development of a joint Franco–British land based long range missile. But negotiations on such a co-operation were postponed in March 1989.[30]

In recent statements, President Mitterrand rejected the concept of flexible response. Would he change his mind if Western Europe tended to a unified political structure? This is an open question. Nonetheless, European Political Cooperation (EPC) has made progress since 1983 when the members of the Atlantic Alliance debated on the deployment of American missiles in several European countries. The Single European Act (SEA) is obliging the more affluent EC member states to reflect on the incidence of free trade on the freedom of capital movements and of the latter on the need for a single currency. An area endowed with a single currency would, eventually, consider a common defence, more specifically a European pillar in the Atlantic Alliance.

This chain of considerations from a Europe of the states to a federation of sorts may be day-dreaming. It proves at least that there will be no European pillar in the making as long as the three key European countries have not manifested a common will to build a single market for conventional armaments and to elaborate a coherent European nuclear strategy.

The conclusion is that the European pillar is a far distant possibility and that the objectives deriving from the different positions of the three major countries regarding the Alliance structure (in or out of the NATO integrated command), the type and strategy of armaments (nuclear or non-nuclear) and the nature and speed of European integration (inter-state co-operation or move in the direction of a federation) are formidable.

> 'If a defence community is the *sine qua non* condition for the formal success of Europe, this will remain problematic as long as there will not be as a preliminary a certain political unity'.[31]

The answer to the question formulated at the start of this chapter as to whether President Mitterrand had, since 1981, reduced the antinomy between the strategy based on the sole defence of the national sanctuary and the strategy based on the Alliance leans on the positive side. The strategy of the national sanctuary is not formally rejected but the concept of 'vital interests' is enlarged. Technical co-operation between France and the NATO integrated command is far from negligible. France has adjusted in due time to the shifts in the United States military doctrine and strategy. But there is no question of France returning to NATO nor sharing the decision to use or threaten to use nuclear weapons. France still plays her own cards in arms procurement. The European pillar has still to be erected but the Single European Act points in the direction of closer economic and possibly political European integration. What remains in doubt is the

'Europeanisation' of French nuclear strategy. The French defence posture, as it now stands, has been modified since 1981, largely under the personal influence of President Mitterrand. It is presently accepted by all French political parties with the exception of the Communist Party.

Regarding the future, one should reflect on the following excerpts of Mitterrand's 11 October 1988 speech:[32]

> 'I desire a united defence for Europe, but I cannot hide the difficulties we meet ... The only point where progress has been made was in the relations between France and the Federal Republic of Germany ... We shall do the utmost to cement a European Pillar in the Alliance ... In 1992–1993, if we have succeeded, we shall be able to take a decisive step to give a real content, and not only an imaginary one, to the common defence of Europe'.

Notes

1. François Mitterrand *Ici et maintenant.* Paris: Fayard, 1980, p. 233.
2. Jacques Isnard 'Le rôle de la Force d'Action Rapide ou le don du sang', *Le Monde*, 2 March 1986.
3. Lothar Ruehl serait nommé secrétaire général du Conseil de Sécurité franco–allemand, les régiments s'installent, *Le Figaro*, 7 September 1988; Quatre garnisons outre-Rhin pour la brigade franco–allemande, *Le Monde*, 10 October 1988.
4. Rafale: Les extraits du rapport; Heisbourg: la décision était mauvaise, *L'Express*, 23 September 1988, pp. 36–38. Déclaration de M. Mitterrand à l'IHEDN, *Le Monde*, 13 October 1988.
5. François Mitterrand *Réflexions sur la politique extérieure de la France.* Paris: Fayard, 1986, p. 95.
6. François Mitterrand 'La Stratégie de la France', interview avec Jean Daniel, *Le Nouvel Observateur*, 18 December 1987.
7. Jean-Pierre Chevènement, entretien avec Jacques Isnard, *Le Monde*, 14 July 1988.
8. Chevènement, *op. cit.*
9. Mitterrand, La stratégie de la France, *op. cit.*
10. Karl Kaiser et Pierre Lellouche *Le couple franco–allemand et la défense de l'Europe.* Paris: IFRI, 1986, p. 321.
11. Georges-Henri Soutou 'L'accord INF, le problème stratégique allemand et la France', *Défense Nationale*, June 1988.
12. André Giraud 'La défense de la France et la sécurité européenne', *Défense Nationale*, May 1988.
13. Bulletin du Crédit National, no spécial 'Défense et industrie', First Quarter 1988.
14. 'Défense: les Français croient en l'Europe', *L'Express*, 17 April 1987.
15. International Institute for Strategic Studies (IISS), Thirtieth Annual Conference, Brighton, England, 8–11 September 1988, Committee 4, 'Western Europe's Strategic Role, Towards a European Pillar', papers by Helmut Sonnenfeldt and by Christoph Bertram.
16. OTAN: Contract de 3 milliards pour Thomson CSF. *Fig–ECO*, 17 June 1989.
17. François Heisbourg, Repenser la doctrine occidentale, interview par Vincent Gérard, *Le Figaro*, 2 March 1988.
18. *Le Monde*, 11 March 1987.
19. Mitterrand 'La stratégie de la France', *op. cit.*
20. François Mitterrand 'Lettre à tous les Français', *Le Monde*, 8 and 9 April 1988.
21. *L'Express*, 4 December 1987.
22. *Politique étrangère* 1/1988.
23. Conference at the Hudson Institute, Paris, June 1988.
24. M. Mitterrand, chef des armées; déclaration de M. Mitterrand à l'IHEDN, *op. cit., Le*

Monde, 13 October 1988; Joseph Fitchett 'Mitterrand Affirms Europe's Defence Ties to US', *International Herald Tribune*, 12 October 1988.

25. James M Markham, France Now Backs NATO Arms Position, *IHT*, 8 September 1988.
26. Charles Lescaut et Claire Tréan 'Les discours de M. Mitterrand à l'ONU, Paris accueillera la conférence sur le désarmement chimique', *Le Monde*, 1 October 1988; Joseph Fitchett, Mitterrand Outlines Arms and Debt Relief Initiatives in UN Speech, *IHT*, 30 September 1988.
27. IISS, *The Military Balance 1987–1988*, Table 5, Global Defence Expenditure Series.
28. IISS, Brighton Conference 1988, Committee 4, Bertram, *op. cit.*
29. IISS, Brighton Conference 1988, Committee 1, Edward N. Luttwak, The Evolution and The Future of Extended Nuclear Deterrence.
30. François Heisbourg, 'Choisir nos armes', *L'Express*, 15 July 1988; Jacques Ismare les projet franco–britannique en missile nucléaire aux calendes grecques, *Le Monde*, 3 March 1989.
31. Francis Cornu, 'Le discours de M. Mitterrand devant l'institute for International Affairs de Londres: De l'Europe du Hasard à l'Europe nécessaire', *Le Monde*, 17 Janvier 1987.
32. Mitterrand, Declaration à l'IHEDN, *op. cit.*

PART 5

Conclusion

CHAPTER 10

Is There Still a Soviet Threat?: A Former Ambassador's Reflections

SIR FRANK ROBERTS

In any dialogue with the Soviet Union we have to know with whom we are negotiating just as in the past we had to know with whom we were confronted. Hitherto we have thought of the Soviet Union mainly in terms of its leaders. Fortunately, I was Ambassador when we had one great change for the better, when we had Khrushchev instead of Stalin. I knew them both. Today we have Gorbachev who, for want of a better word, is another kind of, 'liberal reformer' in the Soviet Union. I think, in a sense, Khrushchev did very much more for the Soviet public than Gorbachev has yet been able to do. He released 8 million of them from Stalin's concentration camps and removed the threat, although not the possibility, of the knock on the door in the night from the KGB. That is an unlikely development in the Soviet Union today but it could still happen and, therefore, it is important for us to think not only about Gorbachev but about the Soviet public as best we can.

There has been much informed discussion, of course, quite understandably, about the Soviet threat diminishing. I think this is a most misleading way to look at things. People talk as if there has been, since 1945, a real Soviet threat to invade the West. I don't think there has ever been such a threat in terms of intentions. I don't think even Stalin, and certainly not Khrushchev, ever intended to invade the West as long as the West retained a certain strength. What they wanted to do was something quite different. This was to change the balance of forces so that they would have much more influence in the West with individual countries. So I don't think the Soviet threat has diminished in any way in terms of intentions. There is more possibility today of negotiating; in terms of capabilities, however, the threat hasn't diminished at all.

Where now do the Soviet people stand in all this? After all, one of the basic questions in this situation is with what kind of a country are we

151

dealing? Is it a country which is likely to become like us? And this is, I think, the great problem. We meet Russians more easily. I meet Russians and I have Russian friends. I like Russians, by and large. And I am delighted that now it is possible, as it was not before, to talk to them in a pleasant and open way. That is to talk to the Russian intelligentsia, or to the Russian KGB officials abroad, who are among the more agreeable people to talk to, because they have a better education, a greater freedom of discussion, and they are not all thugs. But this is not what we are talking about. Do the Russian people underneath regard themselves as being under an appalling autocratic régime and are they longing for political liberty? I don't think so. I don't think there is any sign of it.

The Russians are now far better educated than they were—right through the country; less so, perhaps, in agricultural districts, but as everywhere else, the agricultural population is diminishing steadily. But they are people who at no time in their history, except for a short time after the Revolution, have lived under anything approximating to a democratic system. Russia never had a Renaissance, it never had a Reformation. Russia was based upon Byzantine Orthodoxy. That is a very admirable system in many ways; it is part of our European civilisation. But it has nothing whatsover to do with Western-style political democracy. It never has had. It doesn't have today. This is not at all what Russians aspire to. I don't think in Russia there is any significant body of opinion which is thinking in terms of changing the Communist system for a politically democratic Western liberal system. They would like to see the Communist system working better. To that extent they are behind Gorbachev. They would like to see it bringing more material rewards which they feel, after seventy years, they deserve and have not yet received, except in very marginal areas.

Obviously, the views of an outside observer are suspect and are anyway based on inadequate information. So let me take the greatest Russian writer, Pushkin. Pushkin was writing shortly after there had been one of the very few semi-liberal movements in Russian history. It came from Russian military men, mostly of good family, who had found themselves in Paris in 1815 to which the Tsar's forces had come with others after the defeat of Napoleon. Many went back to Russia with ideas of changing their country. Pushkin was one of them.

In one of his works, Pushkin wrote that there was a great misunderstanding in the West about Russia. There was a basic difference between the Russian approach, by which I mean the Russian people's approach, not only the approach of the Tsar. In other European countries, whatever the practice might be at any time, the state existed for the individual. In Russia, on the contrary, the individual existed for the state. Pushkin made this as a statement of fact, not as an unhappy and unfortunate situation which should be changed. It was just a basic difference which had to be recognised. And that I think has continued and indeed it has been strengthened, under the Soviet régime. Indeed, under Marxism/Leninism, even more than under Byzantine Orthodoxy, the individual exists for the movement, for Marxism/Leninism, and not the other way round.

In our current dealings, therefore, we must realise this fact, and understand that even if Gorbachev's reforms succeed, the Soviet Union is unlikely to develop into a society like our own, with the Russians wishing to develop democratic political institutions similar to ours. I fear we are in for a considerable disappointment because that is not what the Russian people want. I know some people will remind me of some of the Soviet Union's splendid dissidents. I have met some dissidents. I admire many of them, indeed all of them, for their enormous courage, but I don't think many, if any, of them are thinking in terms of political democracy, as we understand it. Certainly, one of the most famous, Solzhenitsyn, whose views resemble those of nineteenth century Slavophiles, thinks the West is pretty badly organised. He is just as critical of the United States and the United Kingdom as he was of the Soviet Union which he left. Sakharov is a different kind of Russian dissident who I admire much more because I think he is much more modern minded. But I doubt if even he would be thinking in terms of our kind of political liberty. Until recently, he supported Gorbachev's reforms, which was all to the good.

I have perhaps over-emphasised this issue of Russian traditional thinking but, in all our negotiations with the Russians, we have to realise that it isn't only the Russian leader of the day we are dealing with but a Russian society which has no desire to become like ours, except in its material advantages. They do want better material conditions of life and that is what Gorbachev realises. He must introduce economic reforms (*perestroika*), largely so that the Soviet Union may remain one of the superpowers of the world with a strong economy and a strong army, but also to give its people more consumer goods and a better standard of living. He has now been in power for over three years. He started with this as his priority. Three years is a short time but there has been no sign whatsoever of change for the better. Just as there has been no sign of any reduction in armaments production, so has there been no sign of any improvement in consumer goods in the shops. In fact, most observers in Moscow—as *The Times* correspondent Christopher Walker felt free to write on his return to Britain—have argued that things if anything are worse. The queues are longer and life more difficult, not less.

One might say that these are the problems of transition and so they are, to some extent, but Gorbachev is going to be judged before very long by the Russian people in terms of whether he has been able to give them more material prosperity. In my time as Ambassador in Russia, under Khrushchev, the people were satisfied with the fact that on the whole things were a bit better this year than they had been the year before. The Americans made the mistake at that time, of putting to the Russians propaganda about American three car households and the rest of their material civilisation. The Russians did not aspire to that. It was beyond all their dreams. They just wanted to have a better life then they had experienced in the 1940s. Now they are getting more demanding. They know rather more of the world. There have been some improvements. The intelligentsia is enjoying much greater freedom of speech. It is still limited and it all comes down from the top. There is no movement from below, except for the occasional dissident, some brave man prepared to go to prison, or into a psychiatric hospital or, somewhat better, into exile, but very sad to be away from the Russian soil, not normally settling down very easily in the West.

Every reform in Russian history has come from the top, whether you go back to Ivan The Terrible dealing with the Boyars to Peter the Great 'Europeanising' Russia or to Lenin bringing to the country which Karl Marx thought least qualified for Communism, the first Communist régime in power since the seventy days of the Paris Commune in 1871. After Lenin came Stalin, further industrialising Russia and improving its defences. All four of them introduced reform from the top, by extremely ruthless methods which were certainly effective. The problem when Khrushchev came along was that, although he'd been a ruthless Stalinist in his youth, he realised that the days for ruthlessness were over. He tried to introduce his reforms with a minium of repression. He was too impulsive and came up against the Party and his former colleagues who, with help from the KGB and the Army, got rid of him. Now Gorbachev is trying to put his reforms through without ruthlessness. I think he'd find it very difficult in present conditions to be as ruthless as Lenin was but, again, in the light of Russian history, it may be impossible to succeed in so ambitious a programme without a measure of coercion. This is what he's up against and in a way this is what we are up against as well.

This isn't the place to move on from Russia and speak of the problems of the rest of the Soviet empire, except very briefly. There is a desire for political independence in Estonia and Latvia and Lithuania, where they experienced this in the inter-war years. There is a desire for more national independence, I don't think political liberty, in the Ukraine. They have experienced the first but not the second before. There is a certain desire for independence in the Caucasian republics but they do pretty well as it is because they are wonderfully skilful at making the best of the Soviet system. There are the religious problems in Uzbekistan and in Soviet Central Asia, with nationalist, but above all Islamic, issues involved. But there is not yet, I think, the problem of wanting major change because, on the whole, the Central Asian Republics have done better economically with the Soviet Union than they did before, even in some respects better than their tribal neighbours in capitalist Afghanistan or theological Iran.

These are all quite different and serious problems but, frankly, this is not the place to discuss them now. I hope I haven't tested the readers' patience with these reminders of the kind of country with which we are negotiating.

Personally, I admire it in many ways but I would be more than surprised, indeed almost disappointed, if Russia suddenly decided to turn its back on its past and strive to become a Western style democracy.

I quoted Pushkin before and I will quote in conclusion the distinguished Yugoslav reformed Communist, Djilas. The issue was the Russian invasion of Prague in 1968 to put down Dubcek's 'liberal' Communist régime. I said that the invasion of a friendly Slav and Communist country should shock people in Moscow. His reply was that some people in Russia, very few, some of his friends, some of mine, would be shocked, but that the overwhelming majority of the Russians would not be. They would regard this as the right way to treat a people who had bitten the hand that fed them, 'just like (he added) you British must have felt when repressing the Indian Mutiny'. He concluded that never in Russian history had there been 'liberal' movements of any significance.

Index